FOUNDATIONS

Design and Technology

Food Technology

KS3

Pauline Parkman
Sue Forshaw
Gemma Alldritt
Paul Anderson
Kay Grey

Nelson Thornes

Published in 2011 by:
Nelson Thornes Ltd
Delta Place
27 Bath Road
CHELTENHAM
GL53 7TH
United Kingdom

11 12 13 14 15 / 10 9 8 7 6 5 4 3 2 1

A catalogue record for this book is available from the British Library

ISBN 978 1 4085 0814 5

Cover photograph: David Taylor/Alamy
Page make-up by Pantek Arts Ltd, Maidstone
Illustrations by Pantek Arts Ltd and David Russell Illustrations
Printed and bound in Poland by Drukarnia Dimograf

Acknowledgements

Photograph acknowledgements: Alamy: p12M (Steven May), p12B
(Greenwales), p13TR (Jochen Tack), p13BR (Realimage), p44B (Mohammed
Ansar), p52 (Coyote Photography), p54TL (Transport Image Picture Library),
p54R (Jack Sullivan), p57T (Chloe Johnson), p57B (Steven May), p64
(sciencephotos), p65T (Steven May), p77T (redsnapper); **Corbis:** p15 (Peter
Ginter); **Food Standards Agency:** p30; **Fotolia:** pviiT, p8, p10T, p10M, p10B,
p13L, p24T, p24B, p25T, p25B, p32M, p32B, p33TL, p35T, p36L, p36BR, p38T,
p39B, p40, p41, p42T, p42M, p42B, p43T, p44T, p45T, p45B, p46T, p46UM,
p46LM, p47T, p47M, p47B, p48TR, p48BL, p49TR, p49MR, p49L, p49BR,
p50T, p50B, p51T, p51UM, p51LM, p51B, p53L, p53M, p53L, p54BL, p56,
p58T, p58B, p62T, p62B, p63, p66, p68B, p69T, p69B, p70M, p72R, p73M,
p74TR, p76T, p76B, p77M, p77B, p79, p80 p81R; **Getty:** p32T (Bruno Vincent),
p65B (Photodisc), p70T (Jacobs Stock Photography); **iStockphoto:** pv, pviiB,
p2T, p2B, p3, p5T, p5B, p9, p11T, p12T, p20, p21, p22T, p22B, p23T, p23B,
p24M, p25M, p32UM, p32LM, p32BM, p33R, p33BL, p35B, p36TR, p37T,
p37B, p38T, p39B, p43B, p46B, p48TL, p48MR, p48BR, p67, p68T, p70B,
p72TL, p72BL, p73T, p73B, p74L, p74BR, p75, p81TL, p81BL; **Science Photo
Library:** p60 (Patrick Landmann); **The Forest Stewardship Council:** p11B.

Text acknowledgements: www.bbc.co.uk: p23.

Contents

Introduction to Food Technology

A

Food Technology

Food Technology is a very important and useful subject because people will always need to eat. Most of us eat at least three meals a day, and supermarkets, cafes and restaurants are packed with food products, which have to be designed and made by somebody. In Food Technology, you will learn the skills needed to design and make these products.

In addition, you will learn about the ingredients that go into food and gain practical cookery skills, which will help you to lead a healthy lifestyle.

The structure of this book

This book is divided into two sections. The first section (Chapters 1–5) takes you through the process of designing a product. This will help you build up the skills that you need to design successful food products. The second section (Chapters 6–8) will help to improve your knowledge of food and teach you the theory behind making food products. Chapter 9 provides some case studies on groups with different dietary needs, designing for others, and product development.

Designing

Throughout your Food Technology course, you will need to understand the different design needs that a product must meet. This will help you to come up with ideas for useful products. You will learn techniques that will help you become a creative designer. These will also help you to present your ideas to others.

A designer must consider how their products might affect others. For example, they might consider whether the ingredients used to make a product are Fairtrade, or whether the product is suitable for a particular dietary need. They must also consider the effect of their products on the environment. For example, how far have the ingredients travelled and can the packaging be recycled?

By reading this book, you will become a better, more creative designer. You will also become more aware of how the food products that you use and make can affect our society and the environment that we live in. In addition, you will learn about the importance of following a healthy, balanced diet and how to design nutritious, well-balanced food products.

Case study

The price of eggs!

Factory-farmed chickens are often crammed into a space no bigger than an A4 sheet of paper. Many people think this is cruel and so avoid buying factory-farmed eggs.

However, these eggs are used in many food products, from ready-meals to mayonnaise. In fact, around 70 per cent of all eggs used in food products are from factory-farmed chickens.

The European Union wants to put a stop to the production of factory-farmed eggs. However, factory-farmed eggs are much cheaper than the free-range equivalent. This means that food products that contain eggs could become more expensive.

- Will consumers be willing to pay the price?
- Can designers think of alternative ingredients?

Making

To turn design work into creative food products, you will need to know all about the ingredients that could be used to make them. You will also need to know about all aspects of food production, including what skills are needed, what equipment is used, how to prepare food safely and how you can test your final product. These are all things that you will learn in Food Technology. You will also learn how products are made in industry, and how to evaluate them successfully so you can suggest improvements or future developments.

... and finally

Food Technology is a very exciting and rewarding subject. It involves a great deal of decision making and practical work, and you will need to plan ahead and become very organised. In your practical and design sessions you will make quality, enjoyable food products. Hopefully, by the end of the course, you will have designed and made a whole range of food products that you can be really proud of. And you will have gained practical food skills and knowledge that will be of great use to you in the future and should be treasured for the whole of your life.

1.1 Food Technology and the design process

The importance of Food Technology

Food Technology has two key aims. These are:

- to build your practical cookery skills and knowledge
- to teach you design and technology skills, such as creativity, organisation and design.

Food Technology will teach you how to make healthy, well-balanced meals safely and hygienically. These are skills that you will require in later life, to stay fit and healthy. Food Technology is also about the development of new food products that could be **manufactured** and sold to the **consumer**. Using the skills and knowledge that you gain in Design and Technology, you will be able to design the creative and original food products of the future.

Food Technology within Design and Technology

As Food Technology is part of Design and Technology, you will be taught how to design and make creative, new and original products. Your new food products should always be designed with a particular **function**, **user** and **need** in mind (use the abbreviation FUN to help you remember this). Your new design work should cover all three.

A Food Technology builds practical cookery skills

Link

For more information about the design processes see **1.2 Reasons for product development**.

Function	What the product will be used for.	A product could be designed for a special occasion, e.g. a birthday cake.
User	Who the product is designed for.	A product could be designed for a particular person, e.g. someone with an allergy.
Need	What need the product will meet.	A product could be designed to meet the needs of someone with a certain allergy, e.g. it might not contain nuts.

The function, user and need of an existing product can change. This might be because of a new situation, a new target user, or a change to a group of users. If an existing food product is adapted or changed to meet the new function, user or need, then a brand new product can be created.

Food manufacturers

When food manufacturers develop new products they follow the design process. As part of this, they will carry out research that might help them to create new products or adapt existing ones. This research might include:

- sourcing new ingredients
- reviewing what is fashionable at the time

B Manufactured food products

- taste testing their competitors' products
- asking consumers about their needs.

It is important that food manufacturers adapt their products to meet any changes in the function, user or need of the products. If a manufacturer doesn't update its products, but its competitors do, then the manufacturer might lose sales and profits.

Case study

Food Technology and health

Currently, about two in five adults in the UK are overweight and a further one in five are obese. Diet-related diseases have become the biggest killers in the UK. Heart disease, diabetes and strokes are all on the increase. The risk of developing any of these diseases can be reduced by eating a healthy, balanced diet.

Because of this issue, consumers are becoming more health conscious. Food manufacturers have responded by introducing low sugar and low fat versions of their existing brands. Low sugar soft drinks are a good example of a product developed in response to this change in the needs of the user.

Can you think of any other current issues that could affect the function, user or need of a food product?

Food Technology and skills

Even if you don't want to work in the food industry, Food Technology can still have an impact on your daily life. In the past, most people learnt to cook at home. Because of changes in lifestyles, this does not always happen now, so studying Food Technology is important because it:

- teaches you the skills you need in order to cook a range of recipes safely
- develops core practical skills
- increases your knowledge about food.

If you can make your own food from fresh ingredients, rather than using ready-made or processed ingredients, this will help you to lead a healthier lifestyle.

Activities

1 What skills do you expect to learn in Food Technology? Create a word web of all the skills you might learn. You could include recipes you might learn to cook.

2 Which of these skills do you think you might learn in other Technology subjects as well? Highlight them on your word web.

3 Why do you think these skills are important?

C In the past most people learnt to cook at home

Summary

- Food Technology teaches the practical and creative skills needed to design and make new, creative and nutritious food products.

- New products need to be created in order for food manufacturers to keep their target users interested and make a profit.

The design process

When you are designing a new product, there are a number of things that you have to do. For example, you have to decide what is needed, how to make it and, after making it, test it meets the needs. One way of showing these activities is as a series of tasks. This is referred to as the **design process**. (Figure **A**.)

In practice, the design process is often not carried out in sequence. As you go through it, you find out more about the final product. This can change what was needed at an earlier step. For example, you might find out that you do not have the ingredients that you wanted to use. This might mean that you have to change your design. Sometimes you might have to jump back to an earlier step several times during the process.

Identifying the need

The first step in the design process is to identify the **need**. The need is what the product you are designing must do. A need is a 'problem' that you want to solve. If you write the problem as a positive statement it becomes the need. (Figure **B**.)

It is important to separate needs from wants. A **want** is something that you would **like** the product to have, but the problem could still be solved without it.

```
Identify need
   ↓
Brief
   ↓
Finding out more about what is needed
   ↓
Creating a list of needs
   ↓
Getting some first ideas
   ↓
Improving the ideas
   ↓
Deciding how to make it
   ↓
Making
   ↓
Testing

Evaluation
```

A A design process

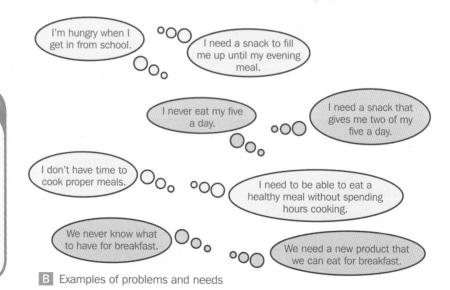

I'm hungry when I get in from school.

I need a snack to fill me up until my evening meal.

I never eat my five a day.

I need a snack that gives me two of my five a day.

I don't have time to cook proper meals.

I need to be able to eat a healthy meal without spending hours cooking.

We never know what to have for breakfast.

We need a new product that we can eat for breakfast.

B Examples of problems and needs

Case study

Ready-made products

In today's society, people have less and less time to prepare meals from scratch. One solution to save people time is a ready-made product that can be reheated and served as part of a meal.

In the UK, pre-prepared frozen food products first became widely available in the late 1970s. At first, ready-made meals were very simple and contained just meat and vegetables. However, there is now a large range of ready-made food products available.

Food manufacturers are under pressure to make sure that the ready-made products they produce are well-balanced and nutritious. Also, they now have to meet a variety of dietary needs: for example, ready-made products that are suitable for a vegetarian or for someone trying to lose weight.

Why do you think there is now such a variety of ready-made products on sale?

Can you imagine how our needs and wants might change again in the future and how ready-made products might develop to meet these needs?

Needs and designing products

A single product might have to meet several different needs. For example, a cupcake for a teenager might have to look appealing, be nutritious and be low in cost. Sometimes meeting one need makes it harder to achieve one of the other needs. For example, when decorating the cupcake you may want to use buttercream icing, because it looks appealing, but find that it is too high in fat. In a situation like this, the designer will have to make a decision about which need is more important.

Another important point about needs is that they can change. This might be because of changes in society or the way we live our lives, or because of developments in technology. For example, in recent years, many food products have been made healthier because consumers have become more aware of the need to eat a healthy, balanced diet.

C Ready-made products have become more sophisticated over time

Link

See **6.7 Dietary needs – age and lifestyle** and **6.8 Dietary needs – a cultural understanding** for more information about the dietary needs of children and vegetarians.

Activities

1 There are more and more vegetarian food products on sale in the supermarket.
   ● What do you think a vegetarian's needs for a ready-made product might be?
   ● What do you think their 'wants' might be?
   Show your ideas in a table like this. Try to explain your answers.

'Needs' of a vegetarian	'Wants' of a vegetarian

2 What other factors might affect the needs and wants a user may have? Thought shower your ideas.

3 What needs and wants might you consider when designing a ready-made meal for children under the age of eight?

Summary

● The design process is the series of activities that are carried out to create a product.

● The first step in the design process is to identify the need.

Understanding the design brief

Objectives

- Be able to explain what a design brief is.
- Be able to analyse a design brief.

What is a design brief?

After a need has been identified, the next activity is to write the **design brief**. This is a short statement of what is needed in a design.

The design brief is given to the person who will design the product. It is often only one paragraph long. A good brief will state:

- what the product must do
- who will use it
- who might buy it, known as the **market** for the product
- the things that limit the design, known as **constraints**
- some important features of the product.

The example below is a design brief for a ready-meal.

This is the need. It is the function that the product must carry out.

This is the market for the product – the people who might buy it. Often this is the same as the user.

This is a constraint – this means it limits what the designer can do. The designer will have to design the snack so that it can be made in a factory.

This is a good example of an important product feature. Remember, food products must look appealing so the user wants to eat them and the market wants to buy them.

Design brief

There is a need for a new snack product for teenagers. The snack would be bought mainly by parents. The cost should be similar to other snack products that are currently available. It should be suitable to be mass produced and sold in the supermarket. It must look appealing to eat. It should contain one of their five fruits and vegetables of the day.

This is the user of the product.

This is another constraint. The designer may have some great ideas for products that would cost too much to make. The designer would have to reject these ideas and choose one that could be made at a lower cost.

This is another important product feature that helps you to begin choosing what ingredients to use in the product.

Analysing the design brief

The next task is to **analyse** the design brief. The aim of this is to identify all the information that you need to know to be able to design the product. This involves asking lots of questions about what is needed, as in the following examples.

- What does the product have to do? How might it do this?
- Who will use it? Who else might be affected by it?
- How will it be used?
- Where will it be used?
- What could it be made from? How could it be made?

You should think about each question in as much detail as possible.

Normally, you will not know all of the answers at this stage. However, this analysis tells you what you need to find out in the next step of the design process.

One way to analyse the brief is to create a 'word web' or spider diagram. This starts with the need in the centre. You then make branches for each question about what is needed. Many of these will have further branches off them, with more questions about the detailed needs of the design. See Figure A for an example.

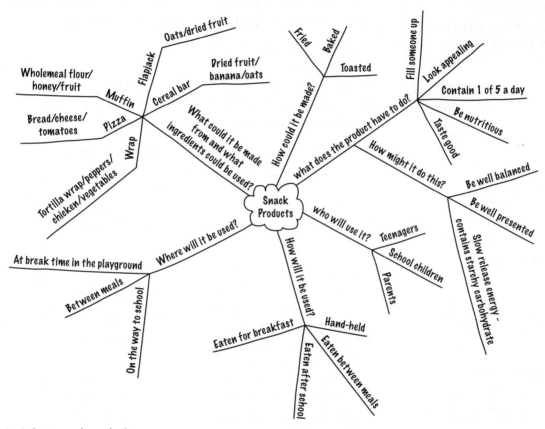

A Wordweb for a snack product

Summary

- A design brief is a short statement of what is required. It should state the user, the market, any constraints and any important features of the product.

- The aim of analysing the design brief is to identify what you need to know to be able to design the product.

Activities

1 Choose a product that you are familiar with. For example, a ready-meal, a pizza or a bag of crisps. Write out the design brief that you think was used for this product.

2 This is the design brief for a product.

   The need is for a fruit-based drink. It would be bought by office workers, teenagers and people 'on the go'. The product should be made to order so that it is fresh, and it should contain at least three different fruits. It should be thick in consistency and provide the user with energy.

   Analyse this brief using a word web.

1.4   Specification

Objectives

- Be able to explain what a specification is.
- Be able to create a specification.

 Link

See **1.3 Understanding the design brief** for more information on analysing the design brief.

Key terms

Specification: a list of needs that the product must meet.

Constraints: something that limits what you can design and make.

What is a specification?

The **specification** is a list of all the needs that the product must meet. Most of the needs in the specification are the answers to the questions identified when the design brief was analysed.

The specification is one of the most important documents created during the design process. It is used to tell us what can and cannot be done when designing the product. If any important needs are missed out from the specification, you might not be able to make the product that you have designed, or it might not do what the users need it to do.

Constraints

It is especially important that any **constraints** are listed in the specification. Constraints are things that limit what you can design or make. For example, if your target user or group was a vegetarian, a constraint would be that your product must not contain meat or meat-based products such as lard. Not all of the needs in the specification will be constraints. Some will be features that users might want, or things that are needed for the product to do what it has to do.

SATSUMAS

A good specification for a simple product might list around 10 needs. **SATSUMAS** can be used to make sure that you have included all the different types of needs in your specification.

A A specification should include the number of people a product could serve

SIZE	What size is the product? How many people will it serve?
APPEARANCE	Does the product look appetising? What colour is it?
TASTE and TEXTURE	What does the product taste like? What texture does it have?
SHAPE	What shape is the product?
UNIT COST	How much does the product cost to buy? Is it good value?
MATERIALS and INGREDIENTS	What ingredients does the product contain?
AGE OF TARGET GROUP	Who is the product aimed at?
STORAGE and SHELF-LIFE	Where should the product be kept? How long can you store it for?

The specification will be used many times during later stages in the design process, for example:

- if there is a choice of possible designs, they might be compared against the specification to see which one is the best
- when the final product has been completed, the design will be compared to the specification to check that it does what it needs to do.

It is a lot easier at those stages if the design can be tested against the needs in the specification.

B A vegetable crumble

Case study

Fruit or vegetable crumble

This is an example of a specification for a fruit or vegetable crumble.

1. It should be family sized and serve at least four people. ← This is a size need.

2. It should have a fruit or vegetable layer topped with crumble. ← This is an appearance, taste and texture need.

3. It should be golden brown and crunchy on the top. ← This is an appearance and texture need.

4. It should contain a seasonal fruit or vegetable with a chunky texture. — This is a taste and texture need.

5. It should be suitable for a family to eat for dessert or as part of a main meal. ← This is a user or target group need.

6. The cost of the ingredients used to make it must be less than £3. ← This is a cost need. It is better to give a range ('less than' or 'from ... to ...') rather than an exact value.

7. It should contain a popular fruit or vegetable to meet the tastes of all the family.

8. It should contain oats in the crumble topping layer. ← These are materials and ingredients needed.

9. It should be freezable. ← These are storage and shelf-life needs.

10. It should last up to three months in the freezer. ←

Activities

1 Create the specification that you think might have been used for a burger. For each need, include a sentence explaining why that need is important.

2 Examine the specification in the case study. Can you add any other specification points to give the designer more information?

3 Attempt to design the product in the specification. Draw out a design idea and label it.

Summary

- A specification is a list of needs that a product must meet. It should include any design constraints.

- SATSUMAS can be used to check that you have covered all the different types of need in your specification.

2.1 Sustainability and environmental impact

Key terms

Non-renewable resources: natural products that will eventually run out and cannot be replaced.

Renewable resources: natural products that are replaced naturally and will not run out.

By-product: product created in the process of making something else.

Pollution: contamination of the environment.

Sustainable materials: materials that are easily available and can be harvested, manufactured and replaced using very little energy.

Food miles: the distance food travels from the farm to your plate.

We are used to having the foods we want to buy and eat, whenever we want them, and at a reasonable price. We are also used to food products having lots of packaging, to protect the food and to encourage us to buy it. Have you ever considered how this lifestyle could be affecting the environment?

How products affect the environment

We should remember that **every** product made has an effect on the environment, both when it is being made and when it is being used.

Making products

Every food product uses a number of ingredients. These ingredients have to be harvested, processed, packaged and transported. All of these processes use materials and energy, and create pollution.

Materials

Packaging is often made from **non-renewable resources** such as oil, which is used to make plastic. 'Non-renewable' means that these resources will eventually run out and cannot be replaced.

The manufacture of food products and their packaging can also produce a lot of waste ingredients and materials that will simply be thrown away.

Energy

Fuel is used to create the energy to cook food products. Currently, most of our energy comes from burning non-renewable fuels such as oil or coal.

In the future, it is likely that more and more of our energy will come from sources such as wind power, solar power (the sun) or tidal power (the sea). These are **renewable resources**. This means that they can be replaced naturally and will not run out.

Pollution

When oil or coal are used to make energy, they do not just make energy, they also produce chemicals and gases at the same time.

These are called **by-products**. If these escape into the environment they can cause **pollution**. One of these by-products is carbon dioxide, which is a cause of global warming.

Using products

Food is produced to be eaten. However, a typical family throws away around £50 worth of food every month! Food packaging, such as plastic trays, plastic bags and cardboard boxes, all gets thrown away too. Some of this waste is burnt and a lot is buried in the ground in landfill sites.

We can reduce the impact on the environment by recycling packaging and using vegetable peelings to make compost.

How can designers make things better?

Food products affect the environment in lots of different ways, from making to disposal. It is important that designers take this into account. They can use the six Rs to help them do this.

Where possible, a designer might think about using **sustainable materials**. These are materials that have less of an impact on the environment because, for example, they are from renewable sources or can be recycled.

Food packaging often has a symbol that shows if it can be recycled. It might also have the Forest Stewardship Council logo, which shows that the cardboard or paper used to make it is from renewable, managed forests. Logos like these help consumers to make informed choices about which products to buy.

Increasingly, food manufacturers are also trying other methods of reducing their impact on the environment. These include:

- reducing the amount of **food miles** by using local ingredients
- not using unnecessary food packaging
- using alternative sources of energy, such as wind power, to help power the factories.

A The recycling symbol

B The Forest Stewardship Council logo

@ Link

See **2.2 The six Rs** for more information on the six Rs.

See **7.5 Food miles and Fairtrade** for more information on food miles.

Summary

- Every product made has an effect on the environment.
- Making food products uses materials – both in making the products and in the waste produced when they are made.
- Making products uses energy. This is often obtained from non-renewable resources.
- Pollution can be caused by the by-products of making a product, or by disposing of a product when you have finished with it.

Activities

1 Food can have an impact on the environment in a range of ways, including waste, air miles and pollution. Produce a word web that analyses all the different ways that food might impact the environment.

2 Choose one of your favourite food products. Using your word web, list all the ways that you think this product could have had an impact on the environment.

3 Write an article for a magazine that explains all the ways in which you could use food differently so as to reduce its impact on the environment. See the Link box for extra help.

2.2   The six Rs

Objectives

- **Be able to list the six Rs.**
- **Be able to explain what is meant by: Recycle, Reduce, Rethink, Repair, Reuse and Refuse.**

A This symbol shows that packaging can be recycled

B Reducing additives means a more natural product that is better for the environment

@   Link

See **7.6 Seasonal and organic foods** for more information on seasonal and organic foods.

C Rethinking might lead you to choose organic vegetables

Every product that is made causes some damage to the environment. Increasingly, both manufacturers and consumers are aware of this impact and are looking for ways to reduce it.

The six Rs are points that a designer and consumer should consider to reduce the impact of their products on the environment.

Recycle

Recycling is a more sustainable way to dispose of food packaging. Metals, glass and many different types of plastic can all be recycled. Packaging that contains materials that can be recycled is often marked to show this, that makes it easier for the consumer to recycle.

Wherever possible, food designers should think about packaging their food in materials that are recycled or can be recycled.

Reduce

Reducing certain aspects of the product and the production process can be better for the environment.

The food designer can:

- reduce the number of food miles used to make the product by using local ingredients
- reduce the amounts of additives or pesticides used to make the product, so it is as natural as possible and does not contain unnecessary chemicals
- reduce waste by reusing leftovers
- reduce the amount of packaging the product uses.

Rethink

Rethink means thinking about all the things that can be done to make the product more environmentally friendly. For example, using organic vegetables because they contain fewer pesticides and other chemicals. Rethinking could completely change the way you buy food products and ingredients.

The designer should also consider the following questions.

- Is the product really needed?
- Could elements of the product be changed to be more sustainable? By using seasonal ingredients, for example.
- Could the product be designed in a different way so that it is more sustainable?

Repair

Repair means mending things so they will last longer. This means that fewer new materials are needed to make replacement products. For example, you could mend a piece of broken kitchen equipment instead of throwing it away and buying a new one. This would save the energy and resources that would have been used to make the new product.

D Repairing kitchen equipment is better for the environment

Reuse

Reuse means using the part again. For example, you can reuse leftovers in your food products. This might be as simple as having your leftovers from your evening meal for lunch the next day. Or you could use the leftovers from a roast dinner to make a new product like a curry or stew. Leftovers such as peelings, cores and egg shells can even be used to make compost for your plants.

Remember

When reusing food products, make sure you follow the correct food safety points.

- Only reheat food once.
- Make sure food is heated to a core temperature of 72°C.

Refuse

Refuse means saying no to things that are harmful to the environment. For example, this might mean refusing to buy food products that use too much packaging, or refusing to buy products that are not grown in the UK.

E Composting is one way to reuse these leftovers

F You might refuse to buy products like these, which use a lot of packaging

Key terms

Recycle: when a product is broken down to make a new product.

Reduce: use fewer resources to make the product, and produce less waste.

Rethink: reconsider the design of the product and the way you use it.

Repair: mending a product so that it lasts longer, or fixing an item when broken rather than throwing away.

Reuse: use waste products again.

Refuse: do not accept things that are not the best choice for the environment.

Activities

1 Design a poster to show how the six Rs are important in the production and use of food.
   - Give a definition of each R.
   - Give at least two food-based examples for each R.

2 Write a letter to the prime minister that explains why you think it is important for designers to be sustainable when it comes to food. You should:
   - discuss the consequences if designers are not sustainable
   - write about any new ideas you have that could make supermarkets follow the six Rs and be more sustainable
   - use facts to support your argument.

Summary

- The six Rs are Recycle, Reduce, Rethink, Repair, Reuse and Refuse.
- By following the six Rs when designing, we can have a positive effect on our environment.

Research

Objectives

- Be able to explain the purpose of research.
- Be able to identify a range of different research activities.

Link

See **1.3 Understanding the design brief** for more information on analysing the design brief.

Key terms

Research: gathering the information you need to be able to design the product.

Primary research: finding out the information you need by yourself.

Secondary research: finding out the information you need by using material that someone else has put together.

Questionnaire: a list of questions used to find out what lots of users want from the product.

Link

See **7.8 Sensory analysis** for more information on sensory analysis.

Why do research?

The purpose of **research** is to gather the information that you need in order to be able to design the product. This means that you need to know what information is required. You will probably have identified this from your analysis of the design brief.

The research you carry out should be relevant and analysed.

- **Relevant** means that you should only investigate the things that you need to know. For example, there would be no point investigating pastry products if your product should contain pasta.
- **Analysed** means that you should draw conclusions from your research. The analysis explains what that piece of research means for your design. For example, each piece of research could be finished with a statement that starts 'As a result of this, I have decided that my product …'

Types of research

There are two main types of research: primary and secondary. **Primary research** is where you find out the information you need by yourself. **Secondary research** is where you use material that someone else has put together. For example, if you were investigating how you might make your product:

- **primary research** might include trying out different methods of making a recipe
- **secondary research** might include using books or watching videos to find out about the processes involved.

Primary research normally takes more time than secondary research. It can be much quicker to read about something than to carry out tests to find out about it for yourself. However, primary research can be focused exactly on the product and information that you are investigating. Secondary research can be very general in nature, although it might still be able to give you the information that you need.

Primary research

Some examples of primary research are:

- using **questionnaires** to ask users what they want your product to do or to look like
- taste-testing existing products – then drawing conclusions about what you liked or did not like, or how the products matched your specification

- experimenting with the ingredients in a recipe – then collecting other people's feedback about what they liked or did not like.

Questionnaires

A questionnaire is a list of questions. It is primary research that is used to find out the needs and wants of the people who will use the product. Ideally, as many users as possible should answer the questionnaire. This helps to make sure that the design will be suitable for lots of people.

Questionnaires usually start by trying to find out if the person answering the questions is likely to use the product. They might ask about age, gender and whether the person already uses the type of product being designed. There will then be a series of questions about each piece of information needed. For example, which ingredients the person likes, how much they might pay for the product, etc.

For each question asked, there will normally be a choice of possible answers. This means that it is easy to plot the answers on to bar graphs or pie charts. These visual tools will help you analyse the questionnaire.

Secondary research

Some examples of secondary research are:

- looking up recipes in a textbook or on the internet
- visiting exhibitions such as the Good Food Show
- interviewing people who know about the subject.

A Sensory analysis taste-testing booth

Questionnaire

Hi, my name is Mike Lloyd and I am going to design and manufacture a portable chessboard that's appealing to the teenage eye. I would be very grateful if you answer a few of my questions.

1. How old are you? (Please tick)
   13-14 ☐ 15-16 ☑ 17-18 ☐ 19+ ☐

2. What gender are you?
   Male ☑ Female ☐

3. How often do you play chess?
   Every day ☐ Weekly ☐ Monthly ☑ Hardly ever ☑

4. What size would you want the chessboard?
   Palm size ☐ Lap size ☑ Desktop size ☑

5. The chess board will be able to compact itself. How would you like it to compact?
   Fold down middle ☑ In a box ☐ Roll up into tube ☐
   Draws for the pieces ☐ Inflatable ☑ Other ....

6. Which material(s) would you like it to be made out of?
   Wood ☑ Glass ☑ Metal ☑ Plastic ☐ Rubber ☑

B Example of a questionnaire

Activities

A supermarket is thinking of designing a new ready-made meal product that is aimed at teenagers. They need to know:

- what ingredients should be in the product
- what culture teenagers would like it to be based on
- what the portion size should be
- when it would be eaten
- how much teenagers would be prepared to pay for it.

1 Design a questionnaire that will find out the answers to these questions.

2 Ask 10 of your classmates to complete the questionnaire.

3 Produce some charts showing your results.

4 Explain what your findings mean for the design of the product. What ingredients should be used, what portion size should it be, etc.

Summary

- The purpose of research is to gather the information that you need to design the product.

- Types of primary research include: using questionnaires, experimenting with ingredients, and examining existing products.

- Types of secondary research include: using books or the internet to look up information, and interviewing people with expert knowledge.

Objectives

- **Understand how to evaluate an existing food product using product analysis.**
- **Understand how this information can help you to design a new food product.**

Link

See **1.4 Specification** for more information on specifications.

Key terms

Product analysis: an existing product is evaluated as a form of research.

Product profile: a chart that displays the criteria of a product on a scale of 0–5. The aim is to get 5 out of 5.

Criteria: properties that your product should have.

Product analysis

When you are designing a new food product, there will usually be existing products that meet similar needs. You can use these existing products as a source of information to help you design your product.

Product analysis involves **evaluating** existing products. It is not just about describing them. It is about understanding why they are designed in the way they are. This is useful because:

- if you identify the good features of the product, you might be able to use these in your design
- if you identify ways that the product could be improved, this might allow you to create an even better product.

Using SATSUMAS

We can use **SATSUMAS**, which we used to write our design specification, to help us evaluate existing products as well. This will help you to identify the good things about the product, but also to identify improvements that could be made to it. This will then help you to create a better product yourself.

SIZE	What size is the product? How many people will it serve?
APPEARANCE	Does the product look appetising? What colour is it?
TASTE and **T**EXTURE	What does the product taste like? What texture does it have?
SHAPE	What shape is the product?
UNIT COST	How much does the product cost to buy? Is it good value?
MATERIALS and **I**NGREDIENTS	What ingredients does the product contain?
AGE OF TARGET GROUP	Who is the product aimed at?
STORAGE and **S**HELF-LIFE	Where should the product be kept? How long can you store it for?

Creating a product profile

Another good way to analyse a product is to create a **product profile** in the form of a star diagram. To do this, choose some positive **criteria** and mark the product out of five against them. You can ask other people's opinions too. The criteria should be quite specific, so that you can easily see how the product could be improved. The criteria could come from your SATSUMAS analysis. Plot your results on your product profile/star diagram.

Case study

An example of a product analysis for a ready-made vegetarian pizza, using SATSUMAS.

SIZE	The pizza is a 25 cm circle in size. This means it can serve at least four people.
APPEARANCE	The pizza is golden brown because of the melted cheese. It has several colourful toppings on, including red and green peppers. You can also see an edge of the tomato sauce topping, which is bright red in colour.
TASTE and TEXTURE	The texture of the pizza is stringy gooey cheese, chunky tomato topping, and a soft bread base. The product has a deep pan base so it is soft in texture.
SHAPE	The pizza is circular in shape and about 2 cm thick.
UNIT COST	The pizza costs £2.99, so it is quite good value for money, costing less than £1 per serving.
MATERIALS and INGREDIENTS	The base is made from flour, yeast, milk powder, salt, sugar and water. The topping is made from tomatoes, citric acid, flavourings, salt and sugar. The toppings are red pepper, mozzarella cheese, cheddar cheese, red onion and green pepper.
AGE OF TARGET GROUP	The pizza is aimed at a family because they can eat it for dinner. This is because of the size of the product. It contains no meat, so could also meet the needs of a vegetarian. The product is not suitable for anyone with a wheat or dairy allergy because it contains flour and cheese.
STORAGE and SHELF-LIFE	The pizza can be stored in the refrigerator for 3–5 days because the packaging states this. It can also be frozen to extend its shelf-life for up to three months. This means it is a convenient food to have at home because it can be cooked from frozen when needed.

Activities

1 Conduct product analysis on a product or piece of packaging in the classroom, or on a product in your lunchbox.

- Firstly, evaluate the product using the SATSUMAS questions.
- Once you have done this, use this information to create a product profile in the form of a star diagram.

2 What improvements could be made to that product based on your product analysis? Explain why you would make those changes.

3 Use this information to draw a design for a new product. Make sure your design work is labelled.

Remember

It is important to say why. A great feature of the product analysis shown in the case study is the use of 'so', 'because' and 'this means', which lead into the explanation of why the product is the way it is.

Summary

- Product analysis is another method of research. It helps you to better understand existing products.
- For it to be successful, it is important that the information is specific and focused.
- The information you get from analysing an existing product can help you to design a new, more successful product.

4.1 Planning

Objectives

- Understand why it is important to plan.
- Be able to create a simple flow chart.
- Be able to list the things that should be included in a production plan.

Link

See **4.2 Ready to cook** for more information on preparation and organisation.

Activity

1 Making a cup of cocoa involves the following activities (not in order):

pour hot milk into cup – get a cup from the shelf – put two spoonfuls of cocoa in cup – stir – heat milk in a pan

- Create a flow chart showing the tasks in the correct order.
- Create a production plan that could be used by someone who had never seen a cup of cocoa being made.

A **production plan** is a set of instructions for making a product. It should contain enough information for someone who has never seen the product before to be able to make it.

Why do we need a plan?

There are lots of reasons why you should plan out what you are going to do!

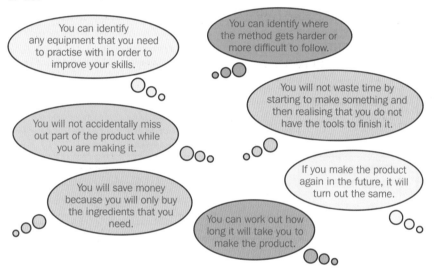

You can identify any equipment that you need to practise with in order to improve your skills.

You can identify where the method gets harder or more difficult to follow.

You will not accidentally miss out part of the product while you are making it.

You will not waste time by starting to make something and then realising that you do not have the tools to finish it.

You will save money because you will only buy the ingredients that you need.

If you make the product again in the future, it will turn out the same.

You can work out how long it will take you to make the product.

At each stage of the process you will know what the next step is going to be, or what is going to happen next, so you will be able to focus on what you are doing.

Deciding how to make the product

The first thing that you need to do is decide how you will make the product. This means that you need to know the ingredients and the processes that you will use.

One way of finding out how to make a product, if you are unsure, is by looking at an existing recipe for a similar product. A recipe will tell you the following information.

- **Product title**: this is name of the product being made. It is sometimes supported with a description line to describe what the recipe is.
- **Ingredients list**: this should show all of the ingredients used in a recipe, and the weights or measurements required for each one.

- **Process**: the process, or method, details the step-by-step instructions to follow to make your product. Sometimes this information is broken down into bullet points or numbers to make it easier to understand.

If you are adapting the ingredients, then you might need to change some of the steps in the method so the tasks are in the right order. For example, if you are adding chicken to a pasta salad, the chicken will need to be cooked before the vegetables to ensure that it is thoroughly cooked. The final order can be shown as a **flow chart** (Figure **A**).

Production plan

In industry, when a product is made, there will usually be lots of steps, or processes, happening at once. These may be carried out by several different people. Therefore a more detailed plan is needed. This is called a production plan.

A production plan takes each step of the process found on a flow chart and adds more detail such as equipment, ingredients and safety points.

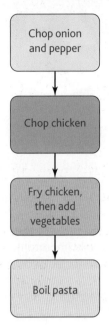

A A simplified flow chart showing the process for making pasta salad with added chicken

Step	Process	Equipment to use	Ingredients to use	Safety notes
1	Dice pepper and onion into small pieces	Green chopping board and sharp knife	Red pepper and onion	Use bridge technique when cutting
2	Chop chicken into small pieces	Red chopping board and sharp knife	Two chicken breasts	Red chopping board used to prevent cross-contamination
3	Fry chicken in wok	Wok	Vegetable oil	Fry chicken until white so you know it is cooked through
4	Add vegetables	Large plastic spoon	Pepper and onion from above	Stir gently so you do not splash oil from the pan
5	Add pasta to a saucepan of boiling water and allow to cook for 12 mins	Saucepan, kettle	Pasta, water	Carefully pour water into pan so you do not scald yourself
6	Drain pasta	Colander	Pasta from above	Carefully pour water from the pan so you do not scald yourself
7	Mix ingredients together	Spoon, serving container	All ingredients from above	

B Example of a production plan for making pasta salad

Key terms

Production plan: the instructions for how to manufacture a product.

Flow chart: a sequence of events presented as a diagram.

Summary

- Planning is important to help you make the product successfully.

- The production plan gives you instructions on how to make the product.

- It should contain all the information needed to make the product, including: the tasks to be carried out, the ingredients, the tools to be used, and safety notes.

4.2 Ready to cook

Objectives

- Understand what steps you should take, before you cook, to be hygienic and organised.
- Understand why these steps are important.

Key terms

Hygienic: preparing and cooking food safely so it does not make anyone ill.

Contaminated: when food contains something it should not contain – from bacteria to hair.

Bacteria: microscopic living things that live on everything around us.

Link

See **8.2 Food safety and hygiene** for more information on food safety and hygiene.

Remember

When using an oven, it is important to wear oven gloves so that you do not burn yourself.

Before you cook

Before you start to cook, you must make sure you are prepared. This means you must:

- **be** hygienic – this means cooking cleanly and safely, so your food is safe to eat
- **be organised** – if you are organised before you start, you can focus on the cooking.

Be hygienic

If you are not hygienic, food can be contaminated by contact with work surfaces, equipment, pests, rubbish, and other foods, such as raw meat. There are bacteria on all of these things. Some bacteria can make you ill if you eat them. This is called food poisoning.

Bacteria also live on your body. So you can easily pass bacteria on to the food. This is why you must be hygienic. Follow these basic steps before and during cooking.

- Wash hands thoroughly with antibacterial soap and hot water before you start cooking.
- Wear a clean apron.
- Do not wear jewellery or nail varnish.
- Long hair should be tied back.
- Avoid coughing, sneezing, or touching your face while cooking.
- Cover all cuts with a blue plaster.
- Wash hands whenever necessary while you are cooking, especially after coughing or sneezing, touching raw meat or using the bin. Also wash your hands when you are changing activities.

Be organised

To be a good cook it helps to be organised before you start. This makes cooking easier, so the product you are making will be more successful. Follow the ready-to-cook checklist.

The ready-to-cook checklist
- Have safety equipment, such as oven gloves, ready to use.
- Have a recipe ready to follow, and read it carefully before you start so you know what you are doing.
- Make sure you have all the equipment and ingredients you need. Check them against your recipe.
- Weigh and measure all ingredients carefully.
- Know how your oven works.

Weighing and measuring

Some recipes must contain the correct amounts of ingredients to be successful. Other recipes can be altered. Recipes where the ingredients need to be weighed correctly are generally for baked products like pastry, bread and cakes. To weigh dry ingredients, use weighing scales or measuring cups. To measure liquids, use a measuring jug. Recipes sometimes use abbreviations for measurements (Figure A).

Abbreviation	Meaning
kg	kilogram
g	gram
ml	millilitre
l	litre
tbsp	tablespoon
tsp	teaspoon

A Recipes sometimes use abbreviations

Activities

1 Make a list of all the ingredients and equipment you might need to make these products.
   - A chicken stir-fry
   - A vegetarian curry
   - A pizza
   - A Victoria sponge cake.

2 Children are being encouraged to learn to cook in primary school. Design a poster or booklet for primary school children (aged between five and seven), which explains what steps they should follow before they start to cook.

Gas mark	Electric °C
1	140
2	150
3	160
4	180
5	190
6	200
7	220

B Gas marks and their °C equivalent

How your oven works

Before you cook, you should find out if you are using a gas or electric oven. Electric oven temperatures are measured in degrees Celsius (°C). Gas ovens are measured in gas mark.

The oven needs to be preheated so it is already hot when you put the food in. You must use the oven temperature your recipe states or your product may not cook correctly. If the temperature is too high, it could burn on the outside and be raw in the middle.

There are three main parts to the oven. Each part of the oven is used to cook food differently.

- **The hob** can be used to boil, steam or fry foods, usually in a saucepan, frying pan or wok.
- **The grill** is used to grill foods such as meat, fish or toast.
- **The oven** can be used to bake or roast foods

C A gas oven

Activity

3 Which parts of the oven would you use to cook the following recipes? State oven, grill or hob.
   - Spaghetti bolognaise
   - Muffins
   - Cheese and potato pie
   - Chicken salad.

Summary

- It is important to be prepared when you are cooking.

- Before you cook you must ensure you are organised and tidy.

- When cooking you should be hygienic to ensure the food you make is safe to eat.

Objectives

- Evaluate your current practical skills.
- Understand how cooking skills can help you lead a healthier lifestyle.

boiling   chopping

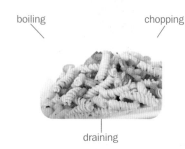

draining

baking   chopping   draining   frying

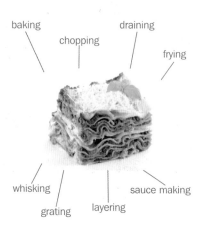

whisking   sauce making   grating   layering

Key terms

Practical skills: the skills needed in order to cook a recipe.

Pre-manufactured: ready-made or processed, for example a ready-made pizza base.

Skills

In Food Technology you will learn how to use a range of **practical skills**. You will probably find some of these skills easy to learn, but others more difficult. You will also find that some recipes use a lot of skills, so can be difficult to follow, whereas others use fewer skills, so are simpler to prepare. For example, a lot more skills are used to make a lasagne than to make a pasta salad.

Activity

Skills audit

1 A skills audit helps us to identify the skills that we already have, the ones that we need to improve on, and the ones that we still need to learn.

Below are some questions on basic practical skills. To check your skills, answer 'yes', 'maybe' or 'no' to each question.

- *Do you know which ingredients should be stored in a fridge, which should be stored in a cupboard, and which should be stored in a freezer?*
- *Do you know how to weigh and measure dry and liquid ingredients accurately?*
- *Do you know how to use a knife safely and how to cut using either the bridge hold or claw hold?*
- *Do you know how to slice, dice and peel safely?*
- *Do you know how to use a grater safely?*
- *Do you know how to prepare meat, fish and vegetables hygienically?*
- *Do you know how to 'rub in'?*
- *Do you know how to shape, cut and roll out dough?*
- *Do you know how to make cakes using different methods?*
- *Do you know how to line a cake tin?*
- *Do you know how to whisk ingredients?*
- *Do you know how to fold ingredients?*
- *Do you know how to light/turn on an oven safely?*
- *Do you know how to use an oven safely?*
- *Do you know how to use a range of cooking methods, including frying, baking, boiling and grilling?*
- *Do you know how to adapt recipes, or use different ingredients, so that recipes are still successful?*

Pre-manufactured ingredients

Over the last 50 years, there have been huge changes in the way we live. Technology has advanced, more women now go out to work, and most people now work longer hours. As a result, many people have never learnt the skills needed to be able to cook. This has become one of the barriers that prevents people from eating a healthy diet.

Supermarkets now sell a range of food products that are **pre-manufactured** and are aimed at people who do not have the skills to make these products themselves.

To simplify the skills you would need to make a lasagne, you could use pre-manufactured ingredients, such as a ready-made white sauce or tomato sauce. However, when food products are pre-manufactured, they sometimes have extra ingredients added to make them last for longer. Or they may have extra seasonings added, such as salt and sugar, in order to improve their flavour. These added ingredients are unnecessary and often unhealthy.

If you make a homemade pasta sauce you can use fresh tomatoes, and add lots of extra flavour by using ingredients such as garlic and herbs instead of adding salt and sugar. You can even add extra vegetables, such as peppers or carrots, which will improve the flavour and make it even healthier.

Link

See **7.9 Homemade or shop-bought?** for more information on the differences between homemade and shop-bought products.

A Pre-manufactured pasta sauce may contain unwanted ingredients

B A homemade sauce like this one is probably healthier and tastier

Case study

Learning to cook

'English teenagers are to receive compulsory cooking lessons in schools. The idea is to encourage healthy eating to combat the country's spiralling obesity rate. It is feared that basic cooking and food preparation skills are being lost as parents turn to pre-prepared convenience foods.'

Can you think of any other reasons why it might be important to learn to cook?

Activities

2 What skills would you need to use to make the following products?
- Blueberry muffins
- A lasagne
- A chicken curry
- A chicken stir-fry.

3 Write an article for your school's newsletter, explaining why it is important for the pupils at your school to learn basic cookery skills.

Summary

- You will learn to use a range of skills in Food Technology.

- These skills will help you to eat a healthy balanced diet, because if you cook your food yourself, you can add less fat, salt and sugar than are generally found in ready-made products.

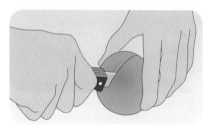

A Bridge method: Fingers should be held together and bent over the product. The knife should cut through the bridge away from the fingers.

B Claw method: Fingers should be held like a claw with fingertips tucked in. The knife will cut up to the knuckles but no further.

Equipment

In Food Technology you will use a range of equipment or **tools**. It is important that you use the right piece of equipment for the job that you are doing. This is so that you can work safely and do the job correctly, which will result in a better quality product.

The following table describes the correct and safe way to use some common kitchen equipment.

Equipment	Function	Safety information
Grater	Used to grate ingredients such as cheese or carrots. Grating cuts the food into much smaller pieces.	• Ensure one hand holds the grater safely when using it. • Do not grate pieces of food that are too small.
Balloon whisk	A balloon whisk is used to 'whisk' air into a food product.	• Remember to hold the bowl steady while you are whisking.
Red chopping board	A red chopping board is used to prepare raw meat.	• Ensure that a red chopping board is only used for raw meat. Other coloured chopping boards should be used for other food products, to avoid cross-contamination. • Ensure that the chopping board is washed thoroughly.

Using a knife safely

It is important that you know how to use a knife safely, so that you do not hurt yourself or someone else.

- Use the right knife for the right job. For example, use a cook's knife for cutting vegetables and a bread knife for slicing bread.
- Use a chopping board to protect the surface.
- Select a knife that is the right size for your hand.
- When carrying a knife, carry it flat by your side.
- When cutting, you should always use either the **bridge method** (Figure **A**) or the **claw method** (Figure **B**).
- If you are having difficulty cutting, the knife might be too blunt. Tell your teacher, because a blunt knife can be just as dangerous as a sharp one. Never touch the blade to check how sharp the knife is!
- Clean the knife as soon as you have finished using it. Never leave a knife in the washing-up bowl.

Measuring equipment

When following a recipe, it is important that you measure the quantities of ingredients accurately, otherwise your recipe might not work properly. There are different pieces of equipment used for measuring different things, including measuring spoons, measuring cups, measuring jugs and weighing scales.

Electrical equipment

There are lots of different types of electrical equipment that can be used during cooking. When you are using this equipment, make sure that the electrical lead is not on the hob or anywhere else where it might cause an accident.

Electric whisk

An electric whisk is a quicker and easier way to beat air into a mixture than a hand whisk. Make sure that the whisk is unplugged when you put the beaters in or take them out. Never start whisking until the beaters are fully in the bowl. When whisking, start on a slow speed. If you start on a high speed, the mixture will fly out of the bowl.

Hand-held blender

This is useful for blending liquid products, such as soups and smoothies. It has a very sharp blade that you should not touch, especially when it is rotating. When using a hand-held blender, do not forget that you also need to hold the container that has the food in it. When you have finished using the hand-held blender make sure that you unplug it.

Food processor

A food processor is useful for blending, grating or chopping ingredients. It can save you time and energy. It has different blades that can be changed depending on what you are using it for. Food processor blades are very sharp, so take great care, especially when cleaning them.

Activity

1 When using a knife, it is important to use it safely so that you do not hurt yourself or someone else. Write eight top tips to follow when using a knife.

C Measuring spoons are useful for measuring small amounts of ingredients, such as herbs and spices

D A measuring jug is used for measuring liquids, such as water or milk

E Weighing scales are used for measuring larger amounts of ingredients, such as flour, sugar and butter

Activity

2 Here are some pieces of basic equipment that you would expect to find in most kitchens: a mixing bowl, a colander, a sieve, a vegetable peeler.

Produce an information page about these pieces of equipment. Draw a picture to show what each one looks like, and then add the following information.

- What each piece of equipment is used for. For example, 'a vegetable peeler is used to take the skin off a carrot'.
- Any safety information that relates to the piece of equipment.
- Some recipes for which you would use that piece of equipment.

Summary

- There is a range of kitchen equipment available.
- It is important to use the right piece of equipment for the job you are doing.
- You must use equipment safely so that you do not hurt yourself or those around you.

5.1   Evaluating ideas

When you have designed a new product, it is essential that you **evaluate** your ideas before you actually make your product. This is to ensure that your product is successful and does what you want it to do. Your ideas should be evaluated to see if there are any changes that can be made to improve your design before you choose your final idea and begin to make your product.

PIN evaluation

A simple method of evaluating your design ideas is by using **PIN**. PIN stands for:

- **P**ositives – state what was good about your design
- **I**mprovements – state what could be improved about your design
- **N**egatives – state what was not good about your design. This can lead to your improvements.

Using the specification to evaluate ideas

If you have completed the initial part of the design process, you will already have come up with ideas about what your product must be or contain. Your specification should draw all of this information together and show what the final product should be.

The most detailed way of evaluating your design ideas is by comparing them with the specification. This is what designers would do in industry.

Design work should be labelled to show how it matches the specification. (See Figure **A** for an example of this process.) You can then check each point of the specification against your design to see if you have covered everything. If something is missing, you can then adjust your design to include it.

Activity

1 Produce another two design ideas to match the specification for the fruit or vegetable crumble.

- Complete a PIN evaluation for each of the two design ideas.
- Adjust the design ideas to show the improvements you have stated.
- If you have no improvements at this stage, then think about how your design ideas could be improved to match the specification.
- Label your ideas to check that they match the specification.

Specification for a fruit or vegetable crumble

1 It should be family sized and serve at least four people.

2 It should have a fruit or vegetable layer topped with crumble.

3 It should be golden brown and crunchy on the top.

4 It should contain a seasonal fruit or vegetable with a chunky texture.

5 It should be suitable for a family to eat for dessert or as part of a main meal.

6 The cost of the ingredients used to make it must be less than £3.

7 It should contain a popular fruit or vegetable to meet the tastes of all the family.

8 It should contain oats in the crumble topping layer.

9 It should be freezable.

10 It should last up to three months in the freezer.

* Design idea one

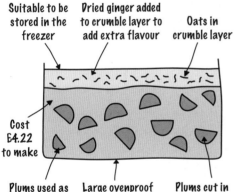

Suitable to be stored in the freezer

Dried ginger added to crumble layer to add extra flavour

Oats in crumble layer

Cost £4.22 to make

Plums used as a seasonal autumn fruit

Large ovenproof dish suitable to fit four portions in

Plums cut in halves to give a chunky texture

* Design idea two

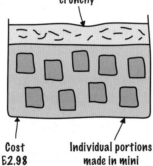

Chopped nuts added to topping to make topping crunchy

Cost £2.98 to make

Individual portions made in mini ceramic dishes

* Design idea three

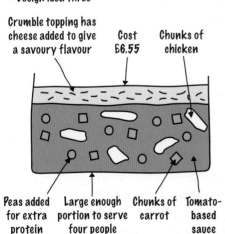

Crumble topping has cheese added to give a savoury flavour

Cost £6.55

Chunks of chicken

Peas added for extra protein

Large enough portion to serve four people

Chunks of carrot

Tomato-based sauce

* Design idea four

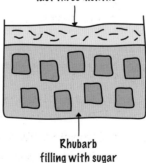

Suitable to be frozen and last three months

Rhubarb filling with sugar

A Specificiation and labelled design ideas for the fruit or vegetable crumble

Activity

2 Check the four design ideas against the specification and identify how you could improve each one.

Summary

● If you evaluate your design ideas, then your final product should be more successful.

● You could complete either a PIN evaluation or a more detailed comparison against your specification.

5.2 Final evaluation

Once you have finished making your product, you will need to check that it meets all of the needs you identified earlier in the design process.

Functional testing

The first step in our **evaluation** of the product is to check that it matches the design brief. One way to do this is **functional testing**. This normally means trying it out. For example, if the design brief was to make a product that was low in fat, you could complete a nutritional analysis on the product to see how much fat it contains. (To be considered 'low in fat', products should contain less than 3 g of fat per 100 g.) Alternatively, functional testing might simply mean taste testing the product.

Comparing the product to the specification

Functional testing does not normally cover all of the needs that the product must meet in enough depth. To evaluate the product more thoroughly you should test it against the specification. This will probably mean that a number of different tests need to be carried out.

Where possible, any testing should be **objective**. This means that it should be based on facts and numbers, rather than opinions. The table in the case study shows an evaluation for a fruit or vegetable crumble. This has a mixture of objective tests and opinions.

Using the evaluation to improve the product

During the evaluation you might identify some needs that have not been met. If this happens, you must explain why. You should also identify what could be improved so that the needs would be met.

Even if your final product meets all the needs, there might still be some things about it that you would like to improve. For example, you may not be happy with the quality of the final product, or there may have been difficulties when you made it. This is to be expected, because your skills and knowledge are improving as you are designing and making products.

You should note down any improvements that could be made. You should explain how any problems or mistakes could have been avoided. In industry, this is very important, because the next person to make the product can use your ideas to improve the product. It will also help you in future practical lessons as you can learn from your own mistakes.

Objectives

- Be able to compare the final product to the specification.
- Be able to use evaluation to identify how the product could be improved.

Link

See **7.8 Sensory analysis** for more information on functional testing.

See **1.4 Specification** for more information on specifications.

Key terms

Evaluation: process of comparing something to a set of standards.

Functional testing: testing by trying the product out, by tasting it, for example.

Objective: based on facts rather than opinions.

Case study

Fruit or vegetable crumble

This is an example of testing against a specification for a fruit or vegetable crumble.

Specification	How tested	Result of testing	Pass/fail
1 It should be family sized and serve at least four people.	It served four people when I took it home.	It was the correct size.	Pass
2 It should have a fruit or vegetable layer topped with crumble.	It contained plums and had a crumble layer on top, which contained oats, dried fruit, butter, flour and sugar.	It contained fruit and crumble.	Pass
3 It should be golden brown and crunchy on the top.	Visual test	It was not golden brown as I did not cook it for long enough.	Fail
4 It should contain a seasonal fruit or vegetable with a chunky texture.	Sensory analysis	The people who ate it said the plum had a chunky texture.	Pass
5 It should be suitable for a family to eat for dessert or as part of a main meal.	Functional testing by my family.	My family enjoyed it for dessert.	Pass
6 The cost of the ingredients used to make it must be less than £3.	Added up the cost of the materials used.	£4.22	Fail
7 It should contain a popular fruit or vegetable to meet the tastes of all the family.	Sensory analysis	My family enjoyed it.	Pass
8 It should contain oats in the crumble topping layer.	Visual testing	It contained oats in the crumble layer.	Pass
9 It should be freezable.	Freezer tests/ Shelf-life quality tests	The product was suitable to be frozen.	Pass
10 It should last up to three months in the freezer.	Freezer tests/ Shelf-life quality tests	Freezer tests proved the product could be frozen.	Pass

Activity

1 Answer the following questions about the evaluation shown in the case study.

- What other questions could be asked in the evaluation? Write a list of five other questions that could be discussed.
- What other tests could be done on the product to check how it matches the specification?
- Which of the tests carried out were objective and which were based on opinions? For each test based on an opinion, either identify a way of testing objectively, or suggest how the specification could be changed to allow objective testing of that need.

Summary

- Functional testing should be carried out to make sure that the product works as intended.
- The product should be compared to the specification to check that it meets all of the identified needs.
- You should also identify how the product could be improved.

6.1   The eatwell plate

Objectives

- Be able to analyse your diet and take steps to improve it.

There is a growing awareness about **obesity** among young people, and the risks it poses to their health. Obesity can result in problems such as strokes, diabetes and heart disease in later life.

We all know that we cannot just eat the foods we like because they are not always good for us. Eating the right types of food can help us to maintain a healthy weight. This is why the Food Standards Agency (**FSA**) has developed the eatwell plate.

The eatwell plate is set out in the same way as a pie chart to show, visually, how much of each food group we should be eating every day to prevent excessive weight gain and keep us healthy. It is a visual way of showing the importance of eating a balance of foods from the different food groups.

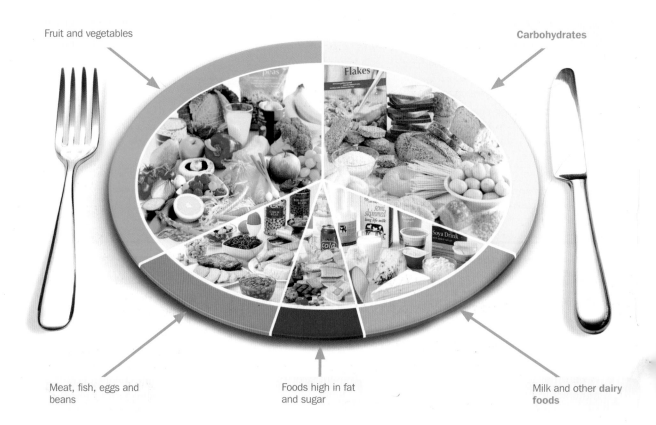

Fruit and vegetables

Carbohydrates

Meat, fish, eggs and beans

Foods high in fat and sugar

Milk and other **dairy foods**

The food groups

There are five main food groups represented on the eatwell plate.

- **Carbohydrate-based foods** give us energy and should make up a third of our diet.
- **Fruit and vegetables** should make up another third of our diet. These provide us with vital nutrients, such as vitamin C, which are needed for overall good health.
- **Milk and other dairy foods** give us protein for growth and repair. We should try to choose low fat versions.
- **Meat, fish, eggs and beans** also provide us with protein.
- **Foods high in fat and sugar** must be seen only as occasional treats and should make up the smallest part of our diet.

Remember

A healthy lifestyle is just as important as a balanced diet. Exercising and staying active will help you maintain a healthy weight.

Activity

1. Write down everything you ate yesterday, including snacks and drinks.

   Draw a chart like the one below and fill in all your foods in the correct section. Some foods you have eaten will fit into more than one column. For example, a ham and tomato sandwich on wholemeal bread would go in the bread column, the fruit and vegetable column, the meat column and the fats column, for the butter.

Carbohydrates	Fruit and vegetables	Dairy foods	Meat, fish, eggs, beans	Sugar and fats

   Compare your day's meals with the eatwell plate. How healthy were your choices? Could you make any small changes to improve your meals?

Summary

- If you eat a selection of foods in the correct proportions suggested by the eatwell plate, you should stay healthy.
- Analysing your meals and making small changes can improve your diet.

Key terms

FSA: the Food Standards Agency: a government body set up to guide the public on food safety issues.

Carbohydrates: foods that are based on starch, such as bread and potatoes.

Dairy foods: foods based on milk, usually from cows, which include butter, cheese and yoghurt.

Objectives

- Know what the eight tips for healthy living are.
- Be able to make healthy choices based on the eight tips.

@ Link

See the NHS website for more information on healthy living.

www.nhs.uk

Key terms

Starch: a type of carbohydrate that gives a slow release of energy.

Saturated fats: fats, usually from animal sources, which raise the cholesterol levels in the blood. This can lead to heart disease and other diseases.

Body Mass Index (BMI): a scale that tells you if you are a healthy weight for your height.

The FSA (Food Standards Agency) has produced eight tips that give practical help and advice about healthy lifestyle choices. They say that as well as trying to eat foods in the correct proportions it is important to:

- eat a variety of food, including fresh and wholegrain choices
- balance intake of food to output of energy, to prevent obesity.

Eight tips for eating well

1 Base your meals on starchy foods. Wholegrain varieties are best. Foods that have lots of **starch** include bread, cereals, rice, pasta and potatoes.

2 Eat lots of fruit and vegetables. Five portions a day is the minimum. A portion is about 80 g, or a handful of the fruit or vegetable. Aim to eat lots of different varieties.

3 Eat fish at least once a week, especially the oily varieties. Oily fish includes tuna, salmon, mackerel, sardines and pilchards.

4 Cut down on **saturated fats**, but remember we still need some fat in our diet. Avoid sugary foods and drinks.

5 Try to eat less salt – no more than 6 g per day. This doesn't just mean adding less salt to food. Many foods already have a lot of salt in them, so check the labels carefully and try to eat low salt versions.

6 Get active and try to maintain a healthy weight for your age. Exercise is just as important as diet for maintaining a healthy weight. You can find out whether you have a healthy **Body Mass Index (BMI)** using the BMI healthy weight calculator on the NHS website.

7 Drink plenty of water – about six to eight glasses per day. Water and other fluids are very important to prevent your body from dehydrating.

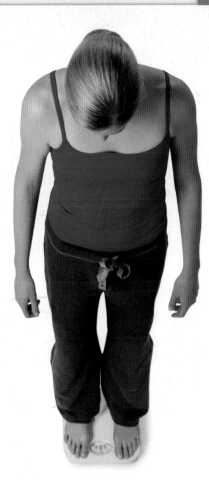

8 Do not skip breakfast or you will miss out on vital nutrients.

Activity

1 Using the FSA or any other relevant website for extra information, design a leaflet aimed at teenagers to promote the eight tips for healthy living.

Case study

Breakfast

All eight tips are important, but many people think breakfast is the key to good health. The word breakfast literally means to 'break the fast', as we should not have eaten for 10 hours before breakfast in order to allow our bodies to rest.

When we are asleep our body functions slow down, for example, our heart rate decreases. In order to get us going in the morning we need slow release energy from foods that contain starch. You need energy so you can concentrate in school and so you can complete physical tasks.

Can you think of some suitable foods for breakfast?

Summary

- It is important to eat a variety of foods in the correct proportions.

- There are some key foods for a healthy diet, such as fruit and vegetables, and oily fish.

- There are some foods that should be limited, such as salt, sugar and saturated fats.

6.3 Energy balance

Objectives

- Be aware of the need to balance the input of food with the output of energy.

Key terms

Kilocalories: the units used to measure the energy value of food.

Lifestyle: the kinds of activities done on a daily basis.

Energy expenditure: this is the amount of energy we use to make our muscles work.

 Link

See **6.1 The eatwell plate** for more on fats and carbohydrates.

Why do we need energy?

Energy from food is needed to keep us alive and active. We need energy for lots of tasks in the body.

- To make our muscles move, in order to carry out physical activities such as walking.
- To keep our bodies at the correct temperature of 37°C.
- To keep our involuntary muscles working. (These are muscles that we do not have to think about using, such as those that control breathing and heart beat.)
- To enable our body cells to grow and repair.

Where does energy come from?

We get energy from food, mainly from fats and carbohydrates. If we eat more food than we need for energy, the excess can build up as fat in our bodies.

On the other hand, if we do not eat enough food to give us energy, then any fat we have stored can be broken down to keep the muscles working, and we may become thinner.

How much energy do we need?

The energy value of food is measured in kilocalories. The amount of energy we need depends on a lot of factors, including age, gender and health. It also depends on our lifestyle – people who are more active need more energy.

On average, boys in your age group should use 2,500 kilocalories a day, and girls should use 2,150 kilocalories. The energy that we use is known as our energy expenditure.

The following table shows you how much energy some everyday activities use.

Activity	Kilocalories per hour
Sleeping	73
Sitting (at the computer, at your desk at school)	80
Standing (in the classroom, in corridors)	110
Light exercise (walking)	277
Moderate exercise (swimming, cycling)	365
Heavy exercise (jogging, tennis, football)	490

Activity

1 Using the table, divide up the activities you did yesterday into one hour chunks, including sleeping. List them, and calculate your energy expenditure. Answer the following points as fully as possible using your findings.

- How close were you to the average energy expenditure for the day for your age group and sex?
- Write two or three sentences on how active you were, detailing how much time you spent being active and how much time you spent resting.
- Think about what you would need to do to increase or decrease your energy output.
- Why do you think boys need more energy than girls?

A Swimming uses around 365 kilocalories per hour

Case study

The Healthy Schools Initiative teaches about all aspects of healthy living, including:

- healthy eating
- physical activity
- emotional health and well-being (including self-esteem and bullying)
- personal, social and health education (PSHE).

The initiative covers all aspects of school life, in and out of the classroom, and provides children and young people with the skills and knowledge to make improved life choices and be healthy.

Is your school a Healthy School? If not, ask your teachers how you can help your school to get that status.

Link

http://home.healthyschools.gov.uk

Summary

- It is important to balance the energy taken in as food with the energy used during daily activities.
- We get the energy we need from food and use what we take in for muscular work. Even sleeping uses energy.
- The Healthy Schools Initiative is helping to make children healthier.

Objectives

- Understand the need for macronutrients in a healthy, balanced diet.
- Be aware of what they do in the body.

Key terms

Pulses: beans, peas and lentils. Foods that use pulses include chickpeas in houmous and kidney beans in chilli con carne.

Empty calories: sugars that provide little or no nutrition, other than energy.

Nutrients are found, in varying amounts, in all foods that come from plants or animals. Macronutrients are the ones the body uses in relatively large quantities: these are proteins, fats and carbohydrates.

Protein

Protein is essential for growth and repair of all body cells and tissues, including blood. It can also be used for energy in an emergency. It is needed throughout life, but especially when we are young, to help growth.

There are two main sources of protein: animal and vegetable. Animal proteins are dairy foods, meat, eggs and fish. Vegetable proteins are **pulses**, seeds, nuts and cereals.

A Animal proteins

Fats

The energy value of fats is worth twice that of carbohydrates. Fat is a concentrated source of energy that also protects our vital organs (such as kidneys) and helps to keep us warm.

The substance omega-3 is found in some fats and oils, and especially in oily fish such as tuna and salmon. It is thought to have many health benefits, especially in preventing heart disease.

We should avoid eating animal fats, such as butter, because they may clog up our arteries, which can lead to heart disease in later life. Vegetable oils, such as olive oil, are a healthy alternative.

B Olive oil is a healthy fat

C Butter is an unhealthy fat

Carbohydrates

Half of our energy should come from carbohydrates.

Starch slowly releases energy, which helps to keep our blood sugar levels steady, so that we stay alert and active. Starchy foods include bread, pasta, rice, breakfast cereals and potatoes.

Sugar is another carbohydrate. However, sugars are 'empty calories'. This means that they do not really have any nutritional value, other than providing energy. Only about 10 per cent of our energy intake should be from sugar.

Case study

Dietary fibre

Another carbohydrate, which is not really a nutrient, is dietary fibre or NSP (non-starch polysaccharide). We need about 13 g per day of this in our diet. NSP passes through our gut virtually unchanged and helps to move waste products through it. This helps to prevent constipation, **diabetes** and bowel cancer, as well as reducing the level of cholesterol in our bodies.

Therefore, NSP must be part of a healthy diet choice. It also provides us with a small amount of energy when digested – as well as gas! It is found in wholemeal cereals and fruit and vegetables. Can you think of any high fibre foods that you eat?

Activity

1 In groups, make small quantities of shortbread biscuits using different quantities of sugar and fat. Use a preference test to find out which quantity best balances acceptable taste and a crispy texture, with lowering of sugar and fat content.

Summary

- Macronutrients are vital for growth and the production of energy in the body.

- Some types, such as starch and olive oil, are healthier than others, such as sugar and butter.

- Dietary fibre (NSP), though not strictly speaking a nutrient, is needed by the body as part of a healthy diet.

6.5 Micronutrients

Link

See the NHS website for more information on micronutrients.

www.nhs.uk

Key terms

Deficiency: when there is a shortage of a particular nutrient in the foods we eat.

Carotene: this is a yellow-orange pigment found in fruit and vegetables. It is converted in the body to vitamin A.

Processed foods: bought products where raw ingredients are prepared, cooked and packaged ready to be eaten.

Micronutrients are made up of two main groups: **vitamins** and **minerals**. The body only requires very small amounts of vitamins and minerals but, because many cannot be made by the body, we need to get them from food. We should eat lots of different foods every day to get the mixture of micronutrients we need, or we may end up with a deficiency, which can lead to illness.

Vitamins

Vitamin A
- Needed for growth and healthy skin, and helps us to see in the dark
- Found in dairy foods, eggs, margarine, and as the yellow-orange pigment **carotene** in fruits and vegetables

B complex vitamins
- Needed for release of energy from foods
- Found in yeast extract, cereals, cereal products, meat, eggs and milk

Vitamin C
- Needed for strong bones and teeth, healthy muscles and nerves, to fight illness, and to help our bodies absorb iron
- Found in many fruits and vegetables, including kiwi fruit, strawberries and peppers, and especially in citrus fruits, such as oranges and lemons

Vitamin D
- Needed, with calcium, for strong bones and teeth
- Mostly made in our bodies by the effect of sunlight on the skin, but also found in eggs, oily fish, milk and margarine

Vitamin E
- Helps protect skin, nose and throat, and against heart disease
- Found in peanuts, seeds and vegetable oils

Vitamin K
- Helps blood to clot
- Found in most foods, but especially green leafy vegetables

Minerals

Calcium
- Needed to help form strong bones and teeth
- Found in dairy foods, bread, cereals, hard water, and canned fish where you eat the bones, such as salmon and sardines

Fluorine
- Strengthens teeth against decay
- Found in fish, tea and water.

Iron
- Forms haemoglobin, the red substance in blood, which carries oxygen to the cells
- Found in liver, kidney, red meat, bread, egg yolk and green vegetables

Sodium
- Maintains water balance in the body and, with chloride, prevents muscle cramps
- Found in cheese, bacon and other salty foods

Activity

1 In pairs, think up a meal – starter, main dish, two vegetables and a dessert – that contains a variety of foods that are good sources of vitamins and minerals.

2 Draw a chart with the **dishes chosen** in the first column, then **vitamins** in the second column, and **minerals** in the third column.

Using the information on this page, and any other relevant sources, list all of the micronutrients that are found in these dishes under the correct column.

3 If there are some that you have not included at all, then write down how you could adapt your chosen meal to include them.

Case study

Salt

Salt is essential to life – all animals need it. However, it can be bad for you if you eat too much, as it can raise blood pressure (hypertension), which can lead to strokes or heart attacks. A normal adult needs only 6 g per day, and it is easy to eat too much. For example, a packet of crisps has 0.14 g and 50 g of corned beef (enough for a sandwich) has 1.1 g. There are lots of ways to cut down on salt, which include:

- avoiding **processed foods**, such as tins and packets, or buying those with no added salt

- not adding extra salt to food

- always checking food labels for salt content

- choosing healthy snacks, like carrot sticks, instead of crisps.

Do you think you have too much salt in your diet? How can you cut it down?

Summary

- Micronutrients are needed in small amounts, but are necessary for all the body's processes.

- They consist of vitamins and minerals, which are found in a variety of foods.

- If we do not have enough of these we will become ill.

Objectives

Objectives

- Understand the link between illness and a poor diet throughout life.

You are what you eat

The foods you eat affect your health, so it is important to think about what you eat. It is especially important during childhood and teenage years, when good or bad eating habits can be formed. Even from a young age, damage can be done to the body that will develop as you go through life and could lead to an early death.

Obesity

Obesity is an increasingly common problem in richer countries because people often eat too much. Obesity is caused by eating more food than the body needs, so that it stores the extra food as fat. It makes people more likely to suffer from health problems such as Type 2 diabetes, coronary heart disease, high blood pressure and joint and muscle problems.

To reverse this growing trend towards obesity, we need to gradually change our diet to one containing lower fat foods, smaller portions and plenty of fresh fruit and vegetables. We also need to make sure we get plenty of exercise.

Remember, you should always consult a doctor before going on a weight-loss diet.

Coronary heart disease (CHD)

CHD occurs when the arteries leading to the heart are blocked by fatty deposits known as cholesterol. If blood cannot get to the heart, a heart attack is likely. CHD results from the modern diet, which is high in saturated fat and processed foods. Try to eat fresh foods rather than processed ones, and avoid saturated fats, which are found in products such as butter, cheese, cream, cakes and biscuits.

Diabetes

Diabetes means that the body cannot control blood sugar levels properly. There are two types of diabetes: Type 1 and Type 2. Type 2 diabetes often results from a poor diet and unhealthy lifestyle. It usually develops in people over the age of 40, but more and more young people and children are getting it, because of poor diet and lack of exercise. It can usually be controlled with a healthy diet and regular exercise. Meal times have to be regular to keep blood sugar levels steady, so it is particularly important that people with diabetes do not skip meals.

Key terms

Obesity: a medical condition where the body has too much fat, and health may suffer as a result.

CHD: heart disease, usually caused by poor diet.

Diabetes: a condition where the body has difficulty converting blood sugar (glucose) to energy.

Anorexia: an illness where people do not eat enough.

Anorexia

Anorexia is a disorder that mainly affects teenage girls and young women. People with anorexia do not eat enough for their age and height for a variety of reasons, often including a fear of getting fat. This means that they become thinner and thinner, and, over time, their hair and skin become dry, and they develop serious health problems such as thinning of bone tissue. If the disorder is not treated, the end result can be death.

Tooth decay

Tooth decay is caused by eating too much sugar. Avoid eating sugary snacks between meals, and brush your teeth twice a day.

Remember

Poor diet not only results in physical effects but also emotional ones, such as low self-esteem. People may turn to 'comfort eating' to make themselves feel better, but this often makes the problem worse.

Activity

SATURATED DISEASE AGE SUGAR HABITS
EAT PROCESSED FOODS FAT BODY
HEART BLOOD PROBLEMS
DEATH MEALS EATING CHD DIABETES
DIET HEALTH FOOD OBESITY
DISORDER

1 Select three key words from the word cloud and find out more about how they relate to a poor diet. Write at least a sentence for each one.

Summary

- You are never too young to start eating a healthy diet.
- Poor diet will result in illness over time. This can be relatively minor, such as tooth decay, or something much more serious, like coronary heart disease, which can result in early death.
- Most of the illness caused by poor diet can be avoided or controlled by making changes to your diet.

Objectives

- Understand how diet needs to change throughout life in order to maintain good health.
- Understand that energy needs vary according to lifestyle.

Key terms

Lifestyle: the kinds of activities done on a daily basis.

There are two main things that affect an individual's dietary needs: age and **lifestyle**.

Age

At different stages in life, nutritional needs are different.

Babies and toddlers

Babies get their nutrition from milk, which can be breast milk or formula. They are then weaned on to solid food, gradually being introduced to different tastes and textures, from soft, pureed vegetables to crisp rusks. Lots of protein, calcium and iron are essential to help growth.

School-aged children and teenagers

Growth increases rapidly at this stage of life, so children and teenagers need lots of protein, calcium and iron. Energy levels also increase, so healthy carbohydrates are essential.

Adults

Growth is in decline, but protein, calcium and iron are still needed for repair of body cells. On the whole, men need more food than women, but in adulthood it is particularly important to consider lifestyle when choosing which foods to eat.

Pregnant women need to eat slightly more than non-pregnant women, and must make sure that they take in lots of nutrients for the developing baby. Especially important are energy foods, protein, all vitamins, calcium and iron.

Older people

As age increases, activity levels tend to slow down. Retirement means that people in this age group no longer need as much energy for work and so do not need to eat as much.

However, there are several vital nutrients that are needed in increased amounts for good health. Older people need plenty of vitamin D and calcium, as bones can break more easily as age increases. Dietary fibre is needed for a healthy gut, and iron is needed to prevent tiredness.

Lifestyle

'Lifestyle' simply refers to the kinds of activities we do on a daily basis. The energy needs of an active person are different from someone who sits down all day. In adulthood, this energy level depends on the type of job you do and your choice of leisure activities. The amounts of energy needed to play darts and run a marathon, for example, are obviously different. Athletes, and other active sportsmen and women, need a high energy intake, mainly from starch. It is important to balance your intake of energy foods with your level of activity.

 Link

See **6.3 Energy balance** for more information about how we use energy.

Activity

1 Design an informative poster, using images from your computer or from magazines, to depict the stages of life and their different nutritional needs. Try to suggest a good breakfast, cooked meal and snack for each age group.

Summary

● Nutritional needs vary throughout life, especially for growth and energy.

● Energy levels vary according to the lifestyle led by the individual.

● At periods of rapid growth, nutrients such as protein and body building vitamins and minerals need to be increased.

Objectives

- Understand about the cultural diversity associated with food.
- Understand the needs of the different cultural groups we have in our society.

Key terms

Multicultural society: a society where people from many faiths and countries of origin live together and share values and food choices.

Cultural diversity: celebrating different cultures and traditions.

Kosher: foods that have been approved for consumption by Jewish law.

Halal: meat eaten by Muslims. The animal is dedicated to Allah and the blood is drained away as part of the slaughtering process.

Britain today is a **multicultural society** with a range of beliefs and values, and this is reflected in the food we all eat.

Some food choices are based on religion, with traditional dishes being eaten at specific times or to celebrate special occasions. Some food customs came about originally as a result of the climate, food availability, cooking facilities and equipment, and income in their country of origin. **Cultural diversity** can include worldwide influences from Europe, to the Indian subcontinent, and beyond.

Supermarkets now stock a huge range of ingredients and ready-made products from all over the world. Consumers often want to try these unusual items. Perhaps they have already tasted them on their holidays. Britain also has a diverse selection of restaurants encouraging us all to try and enjoy different and unusual flavours.

Religion

Many religions have rules about the type of diet they must follow, and this often means that certain foods are banned.

Judaism

Jewish dietary laws and customs are based on ancient Jewish law in the Old Testament. There are many forbidden foods, including pork, shellfish, and eggs with blood spots. Meat has to be ritually slaughtered. Meat and dairy must not be eaten or even prepared together, so orthodox Jewish homes have two kitchen areas. Foods that are approved by Jewish law are known as **kosher**.

A Kosher Jewish bread and wine

Hinduism

The cow is considered sacred in Hinduism, so people of this religion will not eat beef. Strict Hindus are vegetarian, so they tend to eat a lot of pulses and cereals to provide them with protein.

B A traditional Hindu meal

Islam

The pig is considered unclean by Muslims, so no pork or other pig products are eaten. They ritually slaughter their meat so that no blood is left in it. This is known as **halal**.

Christianity

Christianity is better known for its festive foods rather than any dietary restrictions. For example, at Easter, hot cross buns are eaten. The cross is a symbol of Christ's crucifixion, and the fruit symbolises new life.

Some Christians try to eat fish on a Friday, rather than meat. This tradition goes back to the early Christian church, which practised religious fasting on a Friday, the day of Christ's death.

C Halal food products will be marked with a symbol such as this one

Case study

Vegetarians

Many people follow a vegetarian diet because of their religion, but there are several other reasons why people might choose to become vegetarian.

- They might believe that not eating meat is better for the environment.
- They might feel that killing animals is cruel.
- They might believe that killing animals for meat is morally wrong.
- They might believe that a vegetarian diet is healthier.
- They might not like the taste of meat.

There are many types of vegetarians, from the extreme fruitarian, who only eats raw fruit and vegetables, to a demi-vegetarian who may eat fish.

All vegetarians should make sure they have enough protein in their diet with pulses, nuts, cereals and soya products. Do you know anyone who is a vegetarian? Why did they choose this diet?

D Hot cross buns are a traditional Easter food product

Summary

- Britain is a multicultural society with people from many faiths and countries of origin.
- Eating specific foods, or even banning some foods, is an important part of many faiths.
- Vegetarians do not eat meat, for many different reasons.

Activity

1 Carry out some research on a religious festival or celebration.

Write a short paragraph about it, and name some traditional foods eaten during the festival, describing them briefly.

7.1

Types of ingredients

Objectives

- Be aware of the range of ingredients available to produce a variety of food products.

Link

See **7.2 Functions of ingredients** for more information on the functions of ingredients.

Key terms

Staple foods: these are the carbohydrate-based food products that are the main source of starch in a country's diet.

Ingredients

Cooking is a science. Ingredients react differently according to whether they are heated or cooled, and which other ingredients they are mixed with. As a result, they can be combined in endless variety to make different food products.

Milk and dairy products

These are usually from cows, but goat and sheep milks are also used. They are an important source of calcium and protein. Other examples of foods in this group are butter, yoghurt, cheese and cream.

Eggs are another dairy product. We mainly eat eggs from chickens but duck and quail eggs are also available.

Cereal and starchy products

This category includes a huge range of carbohydrate **staple food** products. These are often high in fibre and B group vitamins. The group includes pasta, rice, bread, flour, potatoes and breakfast cereals.

Fruit and vegetables

Fruit and vegetables contain fibre, vitamin C and other water-soluble vitamins. There is a huge variety of fruit and vegetables available, including citrus fruits, bananas, green vegetables, tomatoes and okra.

Meat and fish

The part of an animal where meat comes from affects how tender or tough the meat is. For example, fillet steak is very tender and cooks quickly, but shin beef is very tough and needs long, slow cooking. Fish needs little cooking. Examples of meat and fish include pork, lamb, beef, chicken, haddock and prawns.

Beans, nuts and seeds

Beans, nuts and seeds are often used as the protein source in vegetarian products. Examples include lentils, red kidney beans, Brazil nuts and cashew nuts.

Fats and oils

Fats and oils come from either animal or vegetable sources. They contain fat-soluble vitamins and are a concentrated source of energy. Examples include butter, margarine and olive oil.

Herbs, spices and seasonings

Seasoning is used mainly to make our food taste better rather than for nutritional purposes. Different herbs and spices tend to be used in different parts of the world. For example, basil is used in Italian cookery, lemon grass in Thai dishes and cardamom in Indian dishes.

Case study

Staple foods

Staple foods are the main cereals or starchy foods grown in a particular country or region. This usually depends on the climate. Staple foods form the bulky part of the population's diet, so are the main source of energy and are usually cheap to buy. They become the basis for dishes associated with that country. Examples include:

- wheat: grown in mild climates, and the main staple of the USA, Canada and Europe. In the UK, the staple food product is bread made from wheat.

- rye: grown in colder climates such as Scandinavia and Poland. Examples of its use are rye bread and rye crispbreads.

- maize: grown in hot climates such as southern USA and India, and can be eaten as corn on the cob as well as cornmeal.

- rice: grown in damp tropical areas such as India and China. It has many uses, such as chicken fried rice.

Do you know what the staple food of Ireland is? It is not a cereal crop. You may know some of the history connected to this staple food.

Activities

1 Think of one new example for each type of ingredient, and give a recipe each one is used in.

2 Design a food product that uses as many different types of ingredient as possible. Label your design to show them.

Summary

- There are seven main types of ingredients.

- Ingredients form the basis of all food products.

Functions of ingredients

Objectives

- Understand the different roles played by ingredients in a food product.

All ingredients in a food product have a function. It may be to do with **structure**, taste, texture or appearance, but all have their role to play. These functions are often known as working characteristics.

The 10 main functions are as follows.

Adding flavour

Most ingredients add some flavour, but some are particularly important to the taste of the final product. For example, vanilla in ice cream, chopped basil in a tomato sauce and curry spices in a chicken korma.

Adding colour

Food must be good to look at. Many fruits and vegetables are brightly coloured and will always improve the look of a food product. For example, red and green peppers in a salad and a selection of fruits in a fruit salad.

Adding texture

Crunchy, soft, melt-in-the-mouth – these are all different textures that make our food more interesting. For example, crisp croutons in a soup.

Adding bulk

The bulk is the main ingredient of a food product, as it is present in the largest quantity. For example, flour in bread and rice in risotto.

Setting and thickening

This can be achieved in several ways. For example, flour in sauces, gelatine in jelly, and the setting of eggs in lemon curd.

Aerating

'Aerating' means lightening a mixture with a gas. For example, eggs have the ability to hold air, especially the whites, which can be made into meringue. Other examples include: yeast producing carbon dioxide in bread; chemicals in self-raising flour producing carbon dioxide in cakes; and steam making Yorkshire puddings rise.

Adding nutritional value

All foods have some nutritional value, but sometimes ingredients are added to **enrich** a food product and give it extra nutritional value. For example, egg yolk can be added to both the pastry and the lemon filling of a lemon meringue pie.

Coating

Coating usually involves eggs and breadcrumbs, which can be used to cover or coat a food product before frying. The egg sets, and stops the product getting greasy. For example, the egg and crumb coating on Scotch eggs.

Binding

Eggs are also used for binding, as they set and 'stick' loose foods together during cooking. For example, fishcakes and beefburgers.

Glazing

This is egg or milk applied to the surface of pastry or bread to give a shiny finish when cooked. For example, sausage rolls.

Case study

Garnish and decoration

To garnish a savoury food product is to make it look more attractive. It can be something as simple as chopped chives on a baked potato, or sliced tomato on a cheese and onion flan. Garnishes can add nutritional value as well as colour: for example, vitamin C in tomatoes.

Decoration usually applies to sweet foods, and may include the use of coloured icings, piped cream, fresh or **candied fruit**, chocolate (grated or shaped), chopped nuts, or even gold leaf!

The important thing to remember is that garnishes and decorations should be edible, improve the flavour of the food product and be neatly applied.

Do you think we taste with our eyes first?

Key terms

Structure: the physical shape of a product.

Enrich: literally to make food richer. This can mean adding an ingredient, such as eggs, to add nutritional value to a food product.

Candied fruit: fruit soaked in sugar syrup to preserve it. For example, glacé cherries.

Summary

- All ingredients have a function in a food product; some have more than one.

- These functions help to make the finished product nice to eat.

- All 10 functions are important in making successful food products.

Activity

1 List each of the 10 functions described, then find and name two examples of food products that use that function. Identify the ingredient(s) in those products that perform the function.

Modern ingredients

- Understand the role of modern technology in the development of foods.
- Understand why new food development is necessary for the future.

Key terms

Yield: the amount of food we can get from each plant.

Genetically modified: food in which some genes have been altered in order to improve its properties.

Novel foods: foods developed by humans.

The world population is increasing, so we need to grow more food. People have always tried to improve crop **yield**, for example, through pest control. Now we can also scientifically alter our crops to produce more, better quality food.

The two main types of modern, scientifically altered foods are **genetically modified** (GM) and **novel foods**.

GM foods

Scientists have learnt how to alter genes in plants and animals to improve the properties of our food. This might mean more flavour in a tomato or an increased yield from a crop of maize. Foods that have been altered by this process are known as genetically modified (GM) foods.

All new GM foods are tested carefully to make sure they are safe to eat, and have to be approved by the Food Standards Agency (FSA) before they can be sold in the UK.

This table shows the advantages and disadvantages of genetic modification.

Advantages	Disadvantages
It can increase crop yields, so the crop feeds more people without taking up more growing space.	Because GM foods are new foods, some people are worried that they might have an allergic reaction to them.
It can control certain crop diseases, which may reduce the need to use pesticides.	There are also worries that GM foods could damage our health in other ways that we do not know about yet.
It can increase the nutritional value of the crop and make them more suited to their purpose.	It can be difficult to identify and regulate GM foods, meaning that people could eat them without realising it.

Novel foods

Novel foods are foods that have been developed by humans. It may be the food itself or the processes used to manufacture the food that are novel.

There are several types of novel foods, including:

- **Functional foods** are added to other foods to give specific additional properties. For example, some yoghurts and spreads have plant extracts added, which help to lower cholesterol levels in the blood.
- **Quorn**, or mycoprotein, is a vegetarian protein substitute for meat made from mushrooms. Quorn is high in fibre and low in fat.
- **Encapsulation** traps the flavour of a food in an outer shell to be released later. This process is used to add flavour to jellybeans and crisps.
- **Modified starches** are used to thicken food products when a liquid is added. For example, instant noodles contain modified starch.

Case study

Nanotechnology

Nanotechnology is the manufacture of food and food packaging materials on a minute scale.

Nanotechnology is measured in nanometres. One nanometre is one millionth of a millimetre!

Potential uses of nanotechnology that are being researched and developed include:

- to deliver vitamins or other nutrients in food and drink straight to the blood stream
- to provide a barrier to moisture or gases in food packaging, which would prevent the food drying out or being contaminated
- to enhance the flavour and colour of some foods.

There is great potential, but there are also concerns about their effects on our health.

How do you feel about developments like these? Are you for or against genetic modification and novel foods?

Link

See www.benecol.co.uk

Summary

- GM foods have had their genetic makeup altered for specific advantages or properties.

- A novel food is one that is not found in nature but is usually adapted from one that is. For example mycoprotein is made from fungi.

- Nanotechnology is the latest way scientists are trying to alter the food we eat for specific purposes.

Activity

1 Carry out some research on cholesterol-lowering yoghurts or spreads. (Use the Benecol website)

- How much do they cost? How does this compare with other yoghurts or spreads?
- Who might benefit from these products? What are their health benefits?

Using the information you have found out, create an information sheet on the positive and negative aspects of these products.

Objectives

- Understand that food products come from different sources.
- Be able to explain where we can buy foods from, and why we might choose to buy them from these places.

Link

See **7.6 Seasonal and organic foods** for more information on organic foods.

See **7.5 Food miles and Fairtrade** for more on Fairtrade.

Food is an essential part of our daily lives.

All food products come from either animal or plant sources.

Animal sources

Animals are living creatures. The food products they give us provide valuable **nutrients** that are not as easily available in plant foods, such as proteins. Animal food products include meat and fish, as well as eggs, milk and dairy products.

Animal welfare has become a major concern. The need to produce high volumes of food has led to increased **factory farming**, which some people believe is cruel. Many people will only buy free-range eggs, where the chickens have not been factory-farmed. Another alternative farming method, **organic farming**, is now growing in popularity.

Plant sources

Plants grow in the ground and produce leaves, fruit or seeds that are edible. These are either eaten as they are, or **processed** to make ingredients that can be stored or used to make food products. For example, wheat is used to produce flour, which is then used to make bread, pasta and pastry.

Case study

Knowing where your food comes from

Identifying whether food comes from an animal or a plant is easy when it has been prepared from raw ingredients. However, many food products have been produced in a factory with additional ingredients added so that they stay fresh for longer and are more convenient to store. Sometimes the only way to know if these products contain foods from an animal source is by reading the list of ingredients on the label. However, when we are shopping, we may not have time to read the label on every product. This is why people who do not eat animal products look for the symbol that indicates it is suitable for vegetarians.

There are other symbols on food that are very useful for consumers too.

- The Fairtrade logo shows consumers that the foreign workers involved in producing the product have been treated well and paid fairly.

- The Soil Association organic symbol shows that a food product is organic.

Do you look for any symbols or important information when you buy food products?

Plants produce their crops in different ways. For example, fruit grows on trees and the plant remains for future harvests. However, some crops require a fresh sowing of seeds to produce a further crop. For example, the potato, which grows under the ground, or plants such as cabbage or lettuce, whose leaves we eat.

Processing

Nearly all the ingredients we use to make food products have gone through some form of **processing**. For example, the milk you buy from the supermarket has been processed.

There are two main types of food processing: **primary** and **secondary**.

Primary processing

This starts with raw milk from the farm. This is then heat treated, usually by a method called **pasteurisation**, which helps to keep the milk fresh for longer by destroying harmful bacteria, but does not affect its flavour. The treated milk is then cooled, and some of it is put into bottles or cartons to be sold.

Secondary processing

The dairy then takes the rest of the milk and uses various different processes to turn it into yoghurt, cream, cheese or butter.

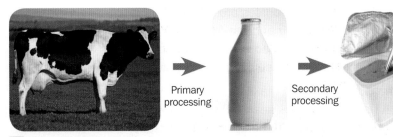

Primary processing   Secondary processing

A Milk processing

Key terms

Nutrients: substances found in food, which the body uses for energy, growth and repair.

Factory farming: raising livestock in confined spaces, because it is cheaper and easier to control them.

Organic farming: growing food and raising animals in a sustainable and natural way, without the use of chemicals or artificial methods.

Processing: taking basic ingredients and changing them in some way to make them more useful, make them safer to eat, help them keep longer, or turn them into complete food products.

Pasteurisation: heat treatment of milk to increase its shelf-life and make it safe to drink, without affecting its flavour.

Activity

1 Pizza contains a range of ingredients including wheat flour, sugar, rapeseed oil, tomato, mozzarella cheese and oregano.

  • List these ingredients and identify whether they come from an animal or a plant.

  • Give details of where each ingredient is grown and how it is produced.

2 Draw a diagram to show how another raw ingredient might be processed.

Summary

● All food comes from animal or plant sources.

● The type of food you buy, and where you buy it, usually depends on your lifestyle and budget.

Objectives

- Understand how transporting food over long distances affects the environment.
- Be able to explain the benefits of choosing Fairtrade products.

Link

See **2.1 Sustainability and environmental impact** for more information on how food products can affect the environment.

A Food is transported to the UK from all over the world

In your local supermarket you can find products from all over the world. Some of these require a different climate to grow successfully. However, some products can be grown in the UK, but are still **imported** because wages and farming costs are lower in other countries.

There are two main issues here.

- The effect that transporting food products across the world has on the environment.
- The poor conditions and pay often faced by the foreign workers producing these products.

Food miles

Food miles are a way of measuring the distance food has travelled from the farm to your plate. All methods of transport produce some carbon dioxide, which contributes to global warming. Therefore, the greater the distance the food has travelled, the more carbon dioxide will have been produced.

The UK is not able to grow all of the food that we eat. Our climate is not suitable, and our resources are limited. As a result, much of our food is transported by air and sea from other countries. Once it reaches the UK, it is then transported across the country by road and rail. All of these forms of transport use oil, a **non-renewable resource**.

As a consumer, you can make a difference by choosing foods grown in the UK or from countries near to the UK. However, some crops grown in heated greenhouses in the UK may be worse for the environment than flying the same product in!

Being aware of these issues will allow you to make informed choices.

Fairtrade

Fairtrade is a term used to describe products that have been grown and produced to a set of agreed rules. These rules make sure that the farmers and producers are treated fairly and that the long term effects of the products on the environment are considered.

B The Fairtrade logo

Many of these farmers and producers live in less developed countries, and the Fairtrade Foundation makes sure that they are paid a reasonable price for the products they produce. An additional payment, called a Fairtrade premium, is also paid, which is used to allow further development of the business.

Fairtrade products are becoming increasingly available in the UK. The most popular products are bananas, coffee, tea and chocolate.

C These workers are harvesting cocoa

Case study

Chocolate bars

There is a high demand for cocoa beans, which are used to make chocolate.

The majority of the world's cocoa is grown on family farms in West Africa, where traditionally the whole family take part in harvesting the cocoa pods from the trees. In some areas of the countryside, the children help with the work. This means that they are not able to go to school, and some of the work they do can be dangerous.

Organisations such as Fairtrade work with the farmers to teach them **sustainable farming methods** and ways of harvesting more crops.

The extra money that is paid for Fairtrade products is used to help the communities. The communities decide what the money should be spent on. It might be used to allow the children to go to school, to provide a well for fresh water, or to invest in training and new ideas for earning money.

By buying Fairtrade chocolate bars, consumers can choose to help others while enjoying their favourite product. As a result of consumer demand, some big chocolate manufacturers now use Fairtrade chocolate.

Key terms

Imported: products brought from another country.

Food miles: the distance food travels from the farm to your plate.

Non-renewable resources: natural products that will eventually run out and cannot be replaced.

Fairtrade: an organisation that makes sure food has been produced in a way that is sustainable and provides a future for the producers.

Sustainable farming methods: those that have less impact on the environment.

Activity

1 The list below shows a selection of typical breakfast ingredients, where they have come from, and the distance they have travelled to London, UK (approx).

Banana	Windward Islands, Caribbean	4,245 miles
Strawberries	Spain	780 miles
Yoghurt	Somerset, UK	164 miles
Porridge oats	Scotland	400 miles
Milk	Lincolnshire, UK	100 miles
Cocoa powder	Ghana, West Africa	3,165 miles
Honey	Mexico	5,556 miles
Tea	India	5,200 miles

- How many miles has this breakfast travelled?
- Identify any of the products have come from overseas that could have been produced in the UK instead. Work out how many miles this would have saved.

Summary

- Knowing how far your food has travelled, and the methods of transportation used, allows you to consider the environmental impact of your choices.

- Fairtrade is an organisation that helps disadvantaged farmers and food producers across the world.

Objectives

- Be able to make informed lifestyle choices based on your knowledge of:
  - how food is grown
  - how the seasons affect the choice of food available.

Key terms

Seasonal: food that has the best flavour and is most plentiful at a particular time of year.

Organic: foods that have been farmed in a sustainable and natural way, without the use of chemicals or artificial methods.

Artificial additives: chemical substances added to food products to extend their shelf-life or improve their colour, texture or taste.

Sustainable: having less impact on the environment.

Inorganic: foods that have not been farmed according to the criteria for organic foods.

Seasonal foods

In the UK, our weather pattern gives us four distinct seasons: spring, summer, autumn and winter. Fruit and vegetables, meat and fish, herbs, mushrooms and nuts are all **seasonal** foods. This means that the food has the best flavour, and the harvest is most plentiful, at a particular time of year.

Because different parts of the world have their seasons at different times, most food products are available somewhere in the world at any time. Many foods are flown into the UK, so they are available to buy even when they are out of season here. For example, we have become used to being able to buy strawberries in December. Strawberries grow naturally in the UK climate producing fruit in the summer months, but in order to have strawberries at other times of the year they have to be flown in from Spain or California.

By choosing food products according to the seasons, it is possible to eat food grown in the UK all year round. There are lots of benefits in doing this.

A Strawberries grow in the UK in summer, but in winter they are imported from other countries

- When a product is in season, it is usually fresher and cheaper than other products.
- You are likely to eat a more varied diet because you will get different foods at different times of year.
- Less energy is needed to produce food when it is in season, and fewer food miles are needed to transport it, so it is better for the environment.
- Buying locally supports your local economy.

Buying seasonal produce is not difficult. For example, many farmers will sell their produce locally in farm shops or door-to-door in boxes. These boxes may include unusual produce that you might not normally buy. So buying locally can introduce you to new foods.

However, if you only buy seasonal produce, then you may not be able to eat your favourite foods all year round, and many consumers are not willing to make this sacrifice.

B An organic, seasonal vegetable box

Organic and inorganic foods

For food to be labelled as **organic**, it must meet certain criteria.

- It must be farmed without the use of chemicals.
- It must not contain **artificial additives**.
- Animals must be cared for in a specific way.
- Farming methods must be **sustainable**.

Organic foods are likely to carry the Soil Association organic symbol.

The term **inorganic** refers to all food products that are not produced to the strict criteria of organic production. For example, they may have been genetically modified, factory farmed, or exposed to chemicals.

The benefits of organic food have not been scientifically proven, but eating organic food is a lifestyle choice made by consumers who are concerned about their health and the environment. Many people also believe that organic foods are of higher quality and taste better. However, they are often expensive and are not always easily available. Therefore, it is difficult for most people to stick to eating only organic foods.

C The Soil Association organic symbol

Activities

1 Create a calendar that shows the different products that are in season in the UK at different times of the year.

2 Compare an inorganic loaf of bread with a similar organic one. You might want to think about the following aspects of the product.
  - Ingredients
  - Nutritional value
  - Cost
  - Taste

  Write a brief paragraph explaining your conclusions and which product you preferred.

Summary

- The climate affects the growing season of crops and their availability.

- Understanding the effects of different farming and production methods allows the consumer to make informed lifestyle choices.

Objectives

- Be able to explain why foods and food products need to be packaged.
- Understand the information on food labels.

Environmental groups are becoming more and more worried about the amount of food packaging we throw away. They want food manufacturers to use less packaging and to make it from materials that can be reused or recycled. However, food packaging is essential for keeping our food fresh and intact.

Why does food need to be packaged?

Protection

- Packaging protects the food from dirt and bacteria.
- Tamper-proof packaging stops anyone from tampering with food. Examples include clicker buttons or paper tapes on jars of jam, and plastic seals around the top of drinks bottles and cartons.

Preservation

- Some packaging can extend the shelf-life of a product. Examples include cans to store fruit or soup, and glass jars for pickles and pasta sauces.

Portability

- Packaging often makes a product easier to transport and store, and prevents it from breaking up. For example, biscuits packaged in moulded plastic trays.

Product recognition

- We often recognise a food product by the shape or colour of its packaging. Also, packaging is usually printed with important information about the product for the consumer.

Packaging materials

The packaging materials used by food manufacturers fall into four main groups: plastics, metals, glass, and paperboard and card.

A Tamper-proof packaging

B Plastic is often moulded to the shape of the food to protect it during transportation and storage

Activities

1 Draw a word web or spider diagram to show the four main groups of packaging materials and a range of foods and food products they are used for.

2 Food manufacturers are often criticised for the amount of packaging they use for their products. About 25 per cent of rubbish in landfill sites is made up of food packaging. What are food manufacturers doing to make their packaging more environmentally friendly? Try to use the following words in your answer: recycle, reuse, biodegradable.

Labelling

Food labelling is controlled by the European Union and must be used by all food manufacturers. This is a **legal requirement**. The following diagram shows the eight pieces of information that must be included on a food label.

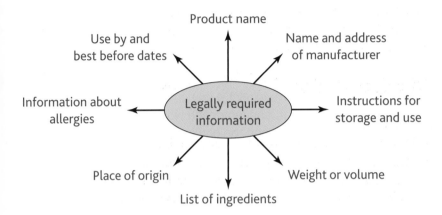

In addition, manufacturers often add extra information to help the consumer. This may include:

- a picture of the product and a more detailed written description
- nutritional information
- the Food Standards Agency traffic light system, which informs consumers about levels of sugar, fat and salt in ready-made products: red for high levels, amber for medium, green for low
- special claims such as 'low fat' or 'high fibre'
- a barcode
- symbols such as 'recyclable' or 'suitable for vegetarians'
- serving suggestions.

Summary

- Packaging protects and preserves food products.
- Where possible, the materials used should be environmentally friendly.
- Materials used for food packaging include paperboard, glass, metals and plastics.
- Food labelling is governed by the EU and eight pieces of information are legally required.

Activity

3 Choose a food product and draw the packaging you would use, including all the necessary information.

Nutrition Facts

Serving Size 3 oz. (85g)

Amount Per Serving	As Served
Calories 38	Calories from Fat 0

	% Daily Value
Total Fat 0g	0%
Saturated Fat 0g	0%
Cholesterol 0g	0%
Sodium 0g	2%
Total Carbohydrate 0g	3%
Dietary Fibre 0g	8%
Sugars 0g	
Protein 0g	

Vitamin A 270%	•	Vitamin C 10%
Calcium 2%	•	Iron 0%

Percent Daily Values are based on a 2,000 calorie diet. Your daily values may be higher or lower depending on your calorie needs:

	Calories	2,000	2,500
Total Fat	Less than	65g	80g
Sat Fat	Less than	20g	80g
Cholesterol	Less than	300mg	300mg
Sodium	Less than	2,400mg	2,400mg
Total Carbohydrate		300g	375g
Dietary Fibre		25g	30g

D An example of a nutritional information label

Five senses

We do not judge food by its taste alone. We can use all of our five senses to test whether we like a food product. This is known as **sensory analysis**.

- Does it **look** appetising? We judge food with our eyes. Is the colour right? Is the food well presented?
- Does it **sound** right? We expect a crunchy biscuit to make a crisp noise when we break it, and lemonade would not be the same without the fizzy sound when the can is opened.
- Does it **smell** appetising? The smell of food makes our mouths water. The bakery in a supermarket or the smell of a freshly cooked burger is difficult to resist!
- Does it **feel** right? How does it feel in our mouths when we are chewing and swallowing it? What texture is it?
- Does it **taste** good? If a food product tastes good we are more likely to buy it again. There are four main tastes that we can recognise: sweet, sour, bitter and salt.

Sensory descriptors

Many people use words such as 'nice' when describing food, but there are a whole range of words, called **sensory descriptors**, which are more specific to food.

Here are some examples of sensory descriptors: **sweet**, **sour**, **herby**, **tangy**, **fruity**, **chewy**, **bitter**, **hard**, **smooth**, **soft**, **greasy**, **fizzy**, **crisp**, **lumpy**, **dry**, **colourful**.

Sensory testing in the food industry

Food manufacturers are always coming up with ideas for new food products, and the best way to decide if the results are good enough is to ask people to try them.

To make the testing fair and accurate, there are certain conditions that must be met.

- The area must be quiet, well lit, and away from other food smells that may affect the flavour of the sample.
- Testers should ideally be separated so they cannot influence each other.
- Small samples of food should be given on identical plates. Paper plates are a good choice.
- Each sample should be given a random code of two or three letters.
- Instructions to testers should be clear and simple, and there should be a prepared chart for them to record their results.
- Water or lime juice should be provided to drink between each sample, to cleanse the palate.

A Food testers trying a new food product

Sensory testing is carried out at various stages of production, and the results are used to change or improve the product according to what people want.

Sensory testing in the classroom

Some of the methods that are used in industry can be adapted for use in your Food Technology lessons. When you carry out your sensory tests, try to use similar conditions to the food manufacturers.

Here is a simple preference test that you can try in the classroom.

- Prepare three similar food samples. These could be ready-made products like biscuits, or items you have made yourself.
- Ask 10 people in your group to taste the foods and fill in a chart like the one below, to show which one they prefer. The testers need to put a tick in the column for the sample they like the best.

The first sample has been done for you and shows that only 1 out of 10 disliked the sample.

	Like a lot 😊	Like a little 🙂	Neither like nor dislike 😐	Dislike a little 🙁	Dislike a lot 😞
Sample XGH	✓✓✓✓✓	✓✓	✓✓	✓	
Sample GHX					
Sample HXG					

Profile test

Profile testing asks a number of testers to grade the characteristics of a product on a scale of 1 to 6, six being the best. The results would be recorded on a chart like this.

Tester	Moist	Sweet	Chewy	Fruity	Golden	Appetising
1						
2						
3						
Total						
Average						

The overall result from the profile test can be worked out as follows.

- Add together the results for each of the characteristics tested. Put this in the **Total** box.
- Divide this total by the number of testers (for the table above this would be three) to find the average for each characteristic. Put this in the **Average** box. This is the final result for each characteristic.

The results for the entire product can be displayed visually on a product profile.

You need to analyse your results to understand likes and dislikes and look at ways to improve your product.

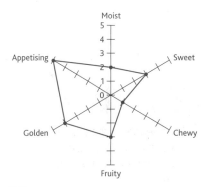

B Product profile for a new biscuit

Homemade or shop-bought?

A Shop-bought muffins individually wrapped

B Homemade muffins

If you were given the choice between a homemade muffin and a shop-bought one, which one you would choose? Several factors might affect your choice.

Appearance

Does one muffin look more appetising than the other? The manufacturer will have considered the presentation of their product very carefully, and the packaging will be designed to make it look as attractive as possible. But, if the recipe and method is followed carefully, a homemade muffin can look even better!

Time

Time has a strong influence on the decision to make or buy.

If the muffins are needed quickly, then buying may be the best option, but you would have to consider the time it would take to go to the shops. Could you make them in the same time at home? Once all the ingredients are weighed and measured, muffins are very quick to make, and they should cook in about 20 minutes.

Nutrition

Homemade products can be healthier than shop-bought, because **you** have control over the ingredients.

Shop-bought muffins are more likely to contain hidden fats and sugars, because manufacturers will usually choose the cheapest ingredients rather than the healthiest.

For example, manufacturers tend to use more unhealthy **saturated fats**, whereas if you make the muffins yourself, you could use a healthier unsaturated fat or oil. You could also reduce the sugar content of a recipe and experiment with wholemeal flour to create a healthier homemade option.

Cost

Shop-brought muffins are likely to cost more than the ones you could make at home. With homemade muffins, the only cost involved would be for the ingredients, and the gas or electricity to cook them.

Shop-bought muffins on the other hand would have to allow for:

- the ingredients
- the bakery or factory with special equipment
- an ongoing programme or research and new ideas to keep up with competitors
- wages to pay the workers
- fuel to heat and light the factory and to cook the muffins
- packaging materials, labels, cost of distribution to shops
- advertising costs
- profit for the manufacturer.

Additives

Food manufacturers are allowed to use **additives** in their products, but these must be listed on the label. Some consumers prefer not to buy products containing chemical additives because they think they are unnatural and unhealthy. Additives are used to:

- extend the shelf-life of the product
- add colour, flavour and texture
- add extra nutrients
- stop some ingredients from separating.

If you choose shop-bought muffins, they are quite likely to contain additives.

However, some of the ingredients for the homemade version might also contain additives. For example, margarine has vitamins A and D added, and flour has a raising agent like bicarbonate of soda added.

Lifestyle

Some groups of people in particular may benefit from choosing shop-bought products. For example, busy working parents who do not always have time to cook, older people who may find it physically difficult to cook, or those who live alone and feel that it is not worth cooking just for one.

However, there is a great deal of pleasure and satisfaction to be gained from planning, preparing and serving homemade food.

C A family enjoying a homemade meal

Case study

Paired comparison tests

In the food industry, one of the sensory tests used when developing new products is called a paired comparison test. Paired comparison tests are used to see which of two products is more popular with consumers and therefore more likely to sell. Testers are given two samples of a similar product and asked which they prefer.

Activity

1 For this activity you will need homemade and shop-bought muffins to compare.

- Cut small samples for tasting, and label them with a code.
- Draw up a simple chart for your testers to tick which sample they prefer.
- Ask 10 people to take part in your test.
- Which sample came out better?

Compare your results with the rest of your class to see whether most people preferred the homemade or the shop-bought muffins.

Link

See **7.8 Sensory analysis** for more information on sensory testing.

Summary

- Factors that affect the choice between homemade and shop-bought products include: appearance, time, health considerations, cost and additives.

- Most people can benefit from shop-bought products at times, but they are particularly useful for single people, older people and busy families.

8.1 Food storage

Objectives

- Understand the importance of storing food correctly to prevent the development of bacteria, and reduce wastage
- Understand the importance of storing foods at the correct temperatures

 Remember

- Try not to pack items too tightly in the refrigerator; you need to leave space for the cold air to circulate.
- Never put hot foods in the refrigerator because the inside temperature will rise and bacteria will start to grow.

A Food products are stored correctly in this refrigerator

It is estimated that in the UK we waste billions of pounds worth of food every year. On average a typical family throws away almost £50 worth of food each month.

The waste food ends up in landfill sites, which has a big impact on the environment and increases the production of greenhouse gases. Much of this wastage is due to food being stored incorrectly, which allows it to break down and become inedible.

Where and how should we store food?

There are three main storage areas in the kitchen: refrigerator, freezer and cupboards.

Which foods should be stored in the refrigerator?
Cold temperatures slow down the growth of bacteria and increase the shelf-life of food. The temperature of the refrigerator should be no warmer than 5°C.

- Any foods bought from the chill cabinet in the supermarket should be refrigerated, such as salads, desserts, milk, yoghurts, cooked meats and ready-meals. It is best to eat these foods by the 'best before' dates given on the packaging.
- Raw meat or fish should be stored in plastic containers with lids, and kept near the bottom of the refrigerator so they do not touch or drip on to other foods. Meat should be used within three days and fish within two days.
- Some jars and bottles need to be refrigerated after opening, for example, mayonnaise, pasta sauces and low-sugar jam. Check the storage instructions on the label.
- Salad ingredients are best stored in the drawer at the bottom of the refrigerator.

Which foods should be stored in the freezer?
The freezer temperature should be no warmer than −18°C.

Freezing does not kill bacteria. They are dormant (asleep) and will start to develop when conditions warm up.

- Most foods can be frozen, except for those that have a lot of water in them, such as salad leaves and strawberries.
- Fresh food should be packed in freezer bags or plastic containers to prevent the surface drying out, which would result in freezer burn.

- When freezing fresh products such as bread, fresh meat or fish, check the label for the freezer symbol or the words 'suitable for home freezing'.
- Frozen foods bought from the supermarket need to be transferred to your home freezer as soon as possible. If possible, transport them home in a cool bag.
- Check the 'use by' date on the labels, and store new purchases behind older ones, so that the oldest food is used first.
- When you defrost frozen meat or poultry, try to thaw it slowly in the refrigerator to prevent it getting too warm.
- Certain foods, such as ice cream, should **never** be refrozen if they have defrosted.

B If you are freezing fresh foods, check the packaging for the freezer symbol

Where should we store everything else?

Most other foods, including all dry ingredients, like flour, cereals, pasta, canned foods, unopened jars and bottles, packet mixes and so on, can be stored in a cool dry cupboard or pull-out larder cupboard. Try to put new items at the back so you use the older food first.

Remember

Try to monitor the temperature of the freezer to make sure it does not get too warm. Some have a thermometer built in but, if not, it is a good idea to buy one.

Key terms

Inedible: cannot be eaten.

Shelf-life: the length of time stored food will keep its quality and be safe to eat.

Freezer burn: grey patches on the outside of food caused by the evaporation of surface moisture. This happens if food is not packaged correctly in the freezer.

Activities

1 Draw a fridge-freezer with the door open and add some sketches to show where and how you would store the following foods.

ice cream   homemade spaghetti bolognese   yoghurt   cheese

milk   eggs   fresh fish   tomatoes   cooked meat

raw meat   orange juice   bread

2 Design a poster or leaflet to give advice on storing food in a freezer. Include lots of colourful sketches to illustrate the points you are making.

Summary

- Storing food correctly can increase its shelf-life and prevent wastage.
- Storing food at the correct temperature is vital: up to 5°C for the refrigerator and −18°C for the freezer.

C Larder cupboard

8.2 Food safety and hygiene

Personal hygiene and food safety

Anyone who handles food needs to make sure that they are hygienic. A few careless mistakes can result in the people who eat the food becoming ill. So, we need to make sure that the rules of hygiene are understood and followed with care, starting with the personal hygiene of the food handler.

Personal hygiene at home and school

Wear an apron. This will protect your clothing and prevent bacteria from your clothes getting into the food.

Cover hair or tie it back. The scalp contains large numbers of bacteria.

Wash hands before handling food and after using the toilet. Bacteria can easily pass from hands to food.

Cover cuts with a blue waterproof dressing. Not many foods are blue, so it can be easily spotted if it falls into the food.

Keep nails short and scrubbed. Bacteria can develop under dirty or chipped nails. No nail varnish, please!

No jewellery. Bacteria like warm moist places, e.g. under a watch strap or bangle.

Personal hygiene in the food industry

In the food production industry, the same rules of personal hygiene apply, but some extra precautions are taken.

- Clean overalls and disposable plastic aprons are worn, and hair is completely covered by a net or cap.
- Hands are washed in an **antibacterial solution** and disposable plastic gloves are worn.
- Blue waterproof plasters have a metallic strip, so they can be found by the metal detector at the end of the production line.
- Any illness must be reported to the supervisor. By law, employees are not allowed to handle food if they are ill.
- Employees working in some areas of the food industry are required to complete a basic food hygiene course.

Objectives

- Understand that good hygiene is important when handling food, in order to prevent the spread of bacteria
- Be aware of safety issues in the kitchen

 Remember

- Do not cough or sneeze over the food.
- Do not lick your fingers or spoons and put them back in the mixture.
- Do not touch your hair, nose or face when preparing food.

Key terms

Antibacterial solution: a liquid that can be sprayed on hands or surfaces to destroy bacteria.

Bacteria: microscopic living things that live on everything around us.

Cross-contamination: the transfer of food poisoning bacteria from one food to another.

Pathogenic bacteria: harmful bacteria that can cause food poisoning.

Kitchen hygiene and food safety

Storing, preparing and cooking are all stages of food production where bacteria may spread and cause disease. We need to take precautions to prevent ourselves and our families from becoming ill with food poisoning.

- Use different coloured chopping boards to prevent cross-contamination. This is when bacteria are transferred from raw food on to cooked food.
- All surfaces and equipment need to be really clean before starting to cook. Use an antibacterial spray if you can.
- The refrigerator and freezer should be kept at the correct temperatures: no warmer than 5 °C for the refrigerator, and no warmer than −18 °C for the freezer.
- Food storage and reheating instructions need to be closely followed. Always keep food covered. Never store raw meat uncovered at the top of the refrigerator, or blood and juices may drip on to food below.
- Waste bins attract flies. Keep them covered and empty them often.
- Try to keep pets out of the kitchen.

In the food production industry a system known as **HACCP** (Hazard Analysis and Critical Control Points) is used to monitor food safety and hygiene.

A Colour-coded chopping boards

Activity

1 What are the main differences between personal hygiene at home and in the food industry?

2 Why do you think the food industry needs to take extra precautions?

How does food poisoning happen?

There are many types of bacteria, and some are very useful, but the ones we must avoid are the pathogenic bacteria that can cause food poisoning. Food poisoning can occur if these bacteria are not destroyed during cooking. Sometimes food is prepared long before it is needed and kept in warm conditions, allowing bacteria to develop. Bacteria will multiply very quickly when given the right conditions – they need warmth, food and moisture to grow.

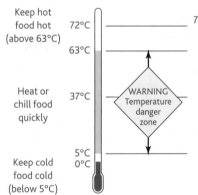

Keep hot food hot (above 63°C) — 72°C — 72°C Bacteria start to be destroyed and are not able to reproduce

63°C

5°C–63°C Bacteria reproduce most actively in this danger zone

Heat or chill food quickly — 37°C — WARNING Temperature danger zone — 37°C Optimum temperature for bacteria to reproduce

5°C
Keep cold food cold (below 5°C) — 0°C — 0–5°C Bacteria are sleeping and reproduce very slowly

−18°C Bacteria are dormant and cannot reproduce

B Critical temperatures for bacteria

Activity

3 In the refrigerator, you find an uncovered plate of raw meat. On the shelf underneath is a trifle, also uncovered. Explain the dangers of this situation and what you need to do to put things right.

4 Why do we need to have different coloured chopping boards? How can they prevent cross-contamination?

Summary

- All food handlers must be aware of the need for good personal hygiene to prevent food poisoning.
- The rules of hygiene must be followed closely when storing, preparing, cooking and serving food.

Cooking methods

When man discovered fire, he also found that some foods were more **tender** and tasted better when they were cooked. Our reasons for cooking food today are very similar.

- Cooking makes foods like meat safer to eat by destroying harmful bacteria.
- Tough food becomes easier to chew and digest after it has been cooked.
- Some foods have a better flavour, texture and appearance when they are cooked.
- Cooking can help to preserve food, for example in jam making.

As a general rule, cooking methods can be grouped into three main categories.

- Moist methods
- Dry methods
- Methods using fat or oil

Moist methods

Boiling can be used to cook most vegetables in a saucepan with a lid. The water should be boiling – which means there are lots of bubbles breaking the surface. Unfortunately, the cooking water is usually thrown away after boiling. This means that nutrients like vitamin C, which leak out from green vegetables during cooking, are poured down the drain.

Poaching is a very gentle way of cooking eggs or fish, and it prevents delicate foods from breaking up. A few small bubbles should appear on the bottom of the pan.

Stewing is a long, slow method that is used for vegetables and tough cuts of meat. They are cooked in a liquid, which is kept at a gentle boil known as **simmering**. Nutritionally this is a good method, because the cooking liquid becomes part of the dish and is not thrown away. Stewing can be done in a saucepan with a lid, or in a casserole dish in the oven. Fruit such as apples, rhubarb or plums can also be stewed.

Steaming is cooking food in the steam that rises from boiling water. It is a very healthy way of cooking vegetables, because the vitamins and minerals do not leak out of the food. Meat, fish, vegetables and sponge puddings can all be steamed.

A An electric steamer

Dry methods

Baking is usually done in the oven, where heat circulates around the food. Many foods are suitable for baking, including bread, cakes, biscuits, pastry, potatoes and pasta dishes. The outside of baked foods is usually crisp and golden brown.

Grilling uses a special flat grill pan with a wire trivet tray inside. This allows any fat to drip through. Grilling is a good method for cooking high fat food like burgers, because the fat drains away making the food more healthy. Foods that might be grilled include tender cuts of meat like steak and chops, fish and, of course, bread to make toast.

B A griddle pan

Methods using fat or oil

Dry frying uses no oil, and the food relies on the fat it contains to prevent it burning. Examples of foods that can be dry fried are bacon and oily fish. Griddle pans with ridges can be used for dry frying. This gives an attractive criss-cross pattern on the cooked food.

Shallow frying uses a small amount of fat or oil, which is preheated before adding the food. Examples of foods that can be shallow fried are tender cuts of meat, fishcakes and eggs.

Deep fat frying is used when the food needs to be completely covered by the hot oil. Electric deep fat fryers are the most popular way of cooking by this method. Deep fat frying is not a healthy method of cooking, because a lot of additional fat is absorbed by the food.

Stir frying is a very quick way of cooking finely cut pieces of meat and vegetables. A small amount of oil is used in a very hot wok, and the food needs to be moved around throughout cooking.

Roasting is where food is cooked in fat or oil in the oven, sometimes in a covered container. It is used mainly for large joints of meat, where the outside becomes crisp and tasty, but it also works well with vegetables like parsnips, squash and sweet potatoes.

Key terms

Tender: easy to chew, not tough.

Simmering: just below the boiling point of a liquid, when bubbles gently break the surface.

Summary

- Food needs to be cooked to destroy bacteria, and to make it easier and more enjoyable to eat, and easier to digest.
- Cooking methods can be grouped into three main categories: moist, dry and methods using fat or oil.

Shopping and budgeting

Objectives

- **Consider the different options available when choosing where to shop**
- **Look at ways to save money when shopping for food**

A A typical supermarket

B Online shopping

Where to shop?

We have plenty of options when it comes to choosing places to shop, and there are advantages and disadvantages for each.

Supermarkets

The range of foods on offer is excellent and prices are competitive. Supermarkets are able to buy food in bulk, and therefore can offer it to the customer at a lower cost. They are also able to sell their own brand products and value ranges at a very low price, by using cheaper ingredients and more basic packaging. This makes it very difficult for smaller shops to compete with them.

The stores are bright and clean and some stay open 24 hours a day. Some supermarkets are sited away from town centres with plenty of parking available. However, this is not good for people without cars. Also, it draws people away from other shops in town centres.

Online shopping

Many supermarkets now provide an online home delivery service. Customers use the internet to view and order the products they need, and the supermarket delivers the goods at a prearranged time. However, customers may have to pay a delivery charge.

It is much easier to resist **impulse buys** when shopping online, but new products and special offers might be missed.

Many people find this method of shopping quicker and more convenient.

Markets and farmers' markets

Markets are popular places to shop for fruit and vegetables. They generally sell locally grown, fresh produce. Some farmers also sell vegetable boxes, which contain a selection of fruit and vegetables, and are delivered to the house every week.

Activity

1 If you buy your vegetables from a market or farmers' market, how might this have a positive effect on:
  - the environment
  - the local economy
  - your health?

  Can you think of any negative effects?

Small local shops

These may be the only option for people who are not able to drive to a supermarket or shop online. People also use the local shop for convenience when they only need a few items. Small shops are limited by their size. They cannot offer such a wide range of goods and because they do not buy in bulk their prices are usually higher.

Specialist shops

Specialist shops sell a particular type of food, but many find it hard to stay in business because of competition from the supermarkets.

Butcher	• Sells raw and cooked meat • Advises on types and cuts of meat and how to cook them • Can remove the bones from meat and prepare meat, e.g. stuffed and rolled joints
Baker	• Sells bread, cakes, pastries and biscuits
Fishmonger	• Sells fresh fish and shellfish • Can give advice on preparing and cooking fish • Will skin and bone the fish if required
Greengrocer	• Sells fresh fruit and vegetables
Delicatessen (or Deli)	• Sells cured meats (like salami), cheeses, pickles, chutneys and other similar products

Budgeting

When shopping for food, it is important to consider how much money is available and set a limit on the amount you can spend.

Here are a few tips to prevent overspending.

- Make a list and stick to it. It is very easy to add impulse buys to your trolley, which can cause you to go over your **budget**.
- Try not to do the food shopping when you are hungry. You will be tempted to buy items that you do not really need.
- Shop around between supermarkets for the cheapest products, and look out for special offers.
- Look out for reductions at the end of the day, especially on **perishable** goods.
- If you have plenty of storage space, buying in bulk can save money.
- Try supermarkets' own brands and value ranges. They are cheaper and can be just as good as well-known brands.
- Be prepared to experiment. Try recipes that use cheaper cuts of meat, for example.

Key terms

Impulse buys: unplanned, spur-of-the-moment purchases.

Budget: a set amount of money you will allow yourself to spend on your shopping.

Perishable: fresh food that will only keep for a short time – fruit and vegetables, for example.

C Impulse buys can come as a shock at the checkout

Activities

2 For each of the following food products, estimate how much you think they would cost.
- A box of six free-range eggs
- A litre of fresh milk
- A pack of four fresh chicken breasts
- A loaf of sliced white bread
- A medium-sized jar of coffee

3 Check your estimates on a supermarket online shopping website. How close were your estimates to the actual price? Were you surprised by the cost of any of the products?

Summary

- There is a wide choice of shops available to the consumer, including supermarkets, small shops, markets and specialist shops. We can also shop online.

- Careful planning and budgeting can save money when shopping for food.

A Developing a cottage pie in the test kitchen

Product development

Food manufacturers are always developing and adapting recipes to create new food products. They must do this in order to keep up with their competitors and adapt to changes in the market. Recipes are developed in a test kitchen, which is very similar to the kitchens we have at home.

In the test kitchen a variety of different samples are made and tested to find the best result. This process is known as **modelling**.

You may have already done some work on product development in your Food Technology lessons. The stages involved are similar to those used in the food production industry.

The changes made to a recipe might include any of the following.

- **Using different ingredients and combinations to create different flavours**: a product such as a cottage pie may be trialled with the following changes to the topping.

Base mixture	Topping
Minced beef, onion, diced carrot	Mashed potato (control)
	Mustard mash
	Parsnip mash
	Sweet potato mash
	Mashed potato with shredded cooked cabbage and spring onion
	Cheesy mash

- **Changing ingredients to fit a dietary need**: if a lasagne product needed to be 'suitable for a low-fat diet', then extra lean minced beef could be used, or a Quorn substitute that is very low in fat. The cheese sauce could be made from skimmed milk and half-fat cheese.
- **Changing the methods used to make and cook the product**: the method of making may be changed according to the skill required and the equipment available, or to make the product healthier. For example, oven baking products like fishcakes, rather than frying them.
- **Changing the cooking temperature or time**: this would be done to alter the colour and texture of the product.

- **Changing the shape**: interesting and unusually shaped products may attract new customers. If the product is designed with children in mind, animal shapes or cartoon characters can often encourage them to eat.
- **Changing the portion size**: a manufacturer may reduce the portion size slightly so that the product can be sold at a more competitive price. On the other hand, an increased portion size would allow the manufacturer to use slogans like 'bigger and better' to encourage people to buy.
- **Changing the nutritional content**: the manufacturer may have seen a gap in the market for a low carbohydrate dessert, so the test kitchen will try reducing the sugar content or using a substitute. Citrus fruit may be added to a dessert to increase the vitamin C content, or calcium may be added to a product by using milk or cheese. These changes to the nutritional content allow the manufacturer to use dietary claims on a product: for example, low fat, reduced sugar, high fibre, and so on.
- **Testing different storage methods**: once a product is completed, different methods of storage may be tried, in order to find the most successful. For example, some products containing sauces can be frozen but sauces may separate out after defrosting. These may need to be sold as chilled products with a much reduced shelf-life, or another type of sauce may be used that contains a **stabiliser** to prevent separation.
- **Using different equipment**: changing the equipment can alter various aspects of the product. For example, using an electric whisk could add more volume to a mixture to make it seem richer. Choosing to blend a vegetable soup rather than leave the vegetables chunky might make it more appealing to children.

B Working on a trial idea

Activity

1 Suggest some changes you could make in the test kitchen to develop a cottage pie recipe. It needs to be suitable for someone who does not eat meat and needs to cut down on fat.

   Take a standard cottage pie recipe as your starting point, then suggest three ways to adapt the recipe, using the nine points given to help you.

Key terms

Modelling: making samples of a product for tasting and testing.

Nutritional content: the amount of protein, fat, carbohydrate, vitamins and minerals that the product supplies.

Stabiliser: a substance added to foods that contain oil and water, to make sure that they stay mixed together properly.

Summary

- A basic recipe can be developed in many different ways to create a new product.
- Product development involves making and testing a product several times to achieve the best result.

Objectives

- Understand the differences between food production methods
- Understand the use of CAD and CAM in food manufacturing
- Be aware of the industrial equipment used in food production

B Batch production system: bread rolls

Key terms

Semi-automated: some of the process is done by machine, but not all of it.

Fully automated: all of the process is done by machine.

Monitor: watch constantly.

Tolerance: the amount of difference in size and thickness that is allowed when manufacturing a lot of the same product.

Food production systems

A large-scale production area is very different from your kitchen at home or school. There are four main food production systems in general use.

One-off production

This is where items are made individually, usually for a special occasion like a birthday or a wedding. A skilled worker is needed for this task and therefore the cost can be quite high.

A One off production: a special occasion cake

Batch production

This is a small-scale production system, such as a local bakery. Large batches of mixture are made and then divided up to make different products. For example, bread dough is made into loaves and bread rolls, and pastry is made into pies, pasties, sausage rolls, and so on. Only a few workers are needed and each may be given a particular task, such as kneading or shaping.

Mass production

This system is used where large numbers of the same product are needed: for example, breakfast cereals or biscuits. The process is **semi-automated**, and computers are used at many stages of the process, therefore fewer food workers are needed.

C Biscuits being mass produced

Continuous flow production

This is a **fully automated**, computer-controlled system, used to make a single product. This method is used to make popular foods such as baked beans or crisps, where large quantities are needed to keep up with consumer demand. The specialised equipment is very expensive and can only be used to make one product.

Quality assurance

Consumers expect a food product to be of good quality every time they buy it. This guarantee of quality is known in the industry as quality assurance. It covers all aspects of food production, including designing, staff training, safety of equipment, record keeping, safe manufacturing processes, packaging and storage.

CAD/CAM

Food manufacturers rely on computers at all stages of designing and making. The use of computers in industry is usually shortened to CAD/CAM.

CAD – computer-aided design

Food product designers use computer software in many different ways to:

- do mathematical calculations for recipes
- calculate nutritional information
- produce charts to **monitor** hazards and safety during production
- design nets for product packaging

CAM – computer-aided manufacture

Computers can be used at every stage of the manufacturing process to:

- weigh and measure ingredients
- chop ingredients to an exact size
- mix ingredients for an exact length of time and at an exact speed
- shape a product accurately, and keep the size and thickness within the agreed **tolerance**
- cook a product for an exact length of time at the correct temperature
- scan for metal objects at the end of the production line
- monitor storage temperatures
- package the finished product

Large-scale equipment

Some items of equipment used in large-scale food manufacturing are similar to ones we use at home or in school. However, others are very different and are designed to do one specific job.

- **Tunnel ovens** are used to cook small items like biscuits. The uncooked food passes through a heated tunnel on a conveyor belt, and cooking is complete when the food appears at the other end.
- **Rotating ovens** are very tall and have rotating shelves to help air circulation and give even browning. They are also used for small items such as Cornish pasties.
- **Enrobing machines** coat a product with another ingredient, for example, melted chocolate to coat a biscuit. A conveyor belt carries the biscuits under the enrobing machine, and any excess chocolate drips through.
- **Depositors** add filling to a container – for example, meat mixture added to a pastry case for a beef and onion pie. The machine adds the exact amount each time.

Activities

1 Which production method would normally be used for each of the following products?
   - cheese and onion crisps
   - 16th birthday cake
   - cornish pasties
   - chocolate digestive biscuits

2 Why do you think the 16th birthday cake would be quite expensive to buy?

3 List the stages where a food manufacturer could use CAM in the making of lasagne. Write a sentence to explain each point.

D Depositor adding ice cream to cones

Summary

- There are four main food production systems: one-off, batch production, mass production and continuous flow.

- Food manufacturers use computer aided design and computer aided manufacture to help them produce safe and attractive products.

- Industrial equipment is designed to do specific jobs in food manufacture.

9.1

Past, present and future

Objectives

- Be able to understand the impact of social and technological changes on the foods we eat.
- Increase your understanding of why people currently lack cookery skills.

Activities

1 What other future developments could affect the foods we eat and the type of food products which need to be designed? Create a word web of ideas. (Look back through the book for suggestions.)

2 What new products could be designed to meet these future developments? Design a new food product to meet the needs of a future development. Make sure your design is thoroughly labelled to explain how it matches the need.

Key terms

Sustainably: having less impact on the environment.

Over the last 50 years, social and technological changes have had a huge affect on the food that we eat and the way it is prepared. The following case study describes the changes that have occurred over this time, and considers how future changes might also affect the foods that we eat.

Case study

The changes

Kitchen equipment

It is amazing to think that most of the equipment that you find in your home or school kitchen were only invented in the last century. The electric kettle was not invented until 1922, freezers were not found in British homes until the 1970s and microwaves did not become common until the 1980s. Now, we rely on these items to make our lives easier. It has completely changed the way we prepare food.

The role of women in the family

In the past, the role of women was to stay at home. However, this has changed dramatically and most women now go out to work. Because of this they do not always want to spend this time preparing food. Also, fewer children are learning practical cookery skills at home, because their mothers do not have the time, or the skills, to teach them.

The development of ready-meals and snack products

Because people now have less time to cook, and most homes have labour-saving kitchen equipment, the need for convenient food products has grown. Food manufacturers and fast-food restaurants have responded to this by designing new products that are quick to cook or ready to eat, such as ready-meals. People now also tend to snack more and eat on the go. Snacks and ready-meals are often heavily processed, and tend to contain more fat, salt and sugar than homemade products.

The impact

There has been a massive impact on society as a result of these changes.

Increase in obesity and diet-related illnesses

The rise in obesity is largely because of modern diets, which contain too many processed foods and too much fat, salt and sugar. Lack of exercise is also to blame. Obesity is linked to the UK's biggest killer: heart disease. It is also linked to other diseases, such as Type 2 diabetes, high blood pressure and osteoarthritis.

Healthy lifestyles and the need to learn to cook

Every school in the UK is now encouraged to teach pupils about a healthy lifestyle. Pupils are taught about the need to exercise and eat healthily, and healthy food is served in school canteens. In addition, all secondary school pupils should be given the opportunity to learn to cook. As well as learning basic cookery skills, pupils are also being taught where to store food, how to shop and how to keep food safe.

It is hoped that this will help to reduce the high levels of obesity in the UK.

The future

More people living alone

An increasing number of people now live alone. This is because of various changes in society, including people starting families later, the breakdown of more marriages, and an increase in the numbers of elderly people living alone, as people live for longer. How might this affect food choices?

Sustainability

The media have made sure that we are all now aware of the impact human beings are having on the planet. This impact can be seen in climate change, landfill and pollution.

As consumers become more aware of this issue they are beginning to act more sustainably. Sales of products such as organic vegetables, free-range eggs and Fairtrade products are increasing.

Health awareness

Because of increasing obesity levels, people are becoming more aware of the need for a healthy diet. Food manufacturers are responding by creating food products that contain fewer additives and less fat, salt and sugar. Evidence of this change can be seen on food packaging and in television commercials for food products.

Food manufacturers are also adding more unusual ingredients, such as soya, wheatgerm, green tea and omega-3, to their products, as they are thought to have specific health benefits.

Summary

- Changes in society and technological advances have changed the way we eat.
- It is essential that food manufacturers are aware of changes in society.

9.2

Designing for others

Objectives

- Understand that different users have different needs.
- Be able to apply your knowledge of designing for others when you design new products.

Designing for others

Different groups of people have different **dietary needs**. You must consider the needs of your target users before you design a product. There are many factors that can affect someone's dietary choices. These include age, diet-related illnesses, religion, culture, and likes and dislikes.

The following case studies will increase your knowledge about the different dietary needs of different groups of people.

Case study

Vegetarians and vegans

A **vegetarian** is somebody who does not eat **any** meat, fish, or shellfish, or any other products that are made by killing animals, such as **gelatine** and animal fats like lard. **Vegans** do not eat any animal products at all, including dairy products and eggs.

People who do not eat any animal products can lack the following nutrients in their diet, so it is important that they eat foods containing these nutrients.

- Vitamin B12 – many vegan foods are fortified with B12, including yeast extract, textured vegetable protein (TVP), soya milk, breads and breakfast cereals.
- Iron – sources include dark green vegetables (such as broccoli and watercress), dried fruits (such as raisins, apricots and prunes), beans, nuts and wholegrains (such as brown rice).
- Vitamin D – the main source of vitamin D is sunlight on our skin. Other sources include fortified breakfast cereals and margarines.
- Calcium sources include dark green vegetables (such as broccoli, kale and cabbage), nuts, soya beans and tofu.
- Protein sources include wholegrains (such as rice, bread and cereals), pulses (such as beans and lentils) and seeds and nuts. These all contain some of the essential amino acids that we need to eat in our diets. Meat substitutes such as TVP and tofu, both made from soya beans, contain all of the essential amino acids that we need.

Key terms

Dietary needs: the foods and nutrients that an individual needs to eat, or needs to avoid eating.

Gelatine: a glue-like substance that comes from animal bones and other animal tissues.

Vegan: someone who does not eat any animal products.

Case study

People with allergies

It is thought that 1–2 per cent of people in the UK have food allergies. The main foods that cause allergies are:

- cow's milk
- eggs
- peanuts and nuts that grow on trees (including Brazil nuts, hazelnuts, almonds and walnuts)
- fish and shellfish (including mussels, crab and shrimps)
- soya
- wheat.

The main symptoms of a food allergy are coughing; dry, itchy throat and tongue; swollen lips and throat; itchy skin or rash; nausea and bloating; diarrhoea and vomiting; wheezing and shortness of breath; red, sore, itchy eyes; runny or blocked nose. Some allergies, in particular nut allergies, can be very serious and can cause fainting, collapse and even death.

Link

See **6.7 Dietary needs – age and lifestyle** and **6.8 Dietary needs – a cultural understanding** for more information on special diets.

Activities

1 Select another dietary group (it could be a religion, or a culture), then complete a PowerPoint or research page on that dietary group. It should explain:
   - what the diet is
   - what the needs of the diet are
   - which foods should or should not be eaten
   - the consequences if that diet is not followed.

2 Design a range of four new products that meet the needs of one of the dietary groups mentioned in the above case studies. Make sure your design work is well labelled so that it is clear how the product matches the needs of the target group.

Summary

- There are many different dietary groups that you may need to consider when you design a food product.
- Dietary needs affect which ingredients go into a product.

Objectives

- **Understand how products can be developed as a result of new technologies or changes to customer needs.**

Even the simplest of food products can be adapted and changed. This might be because of the **market push** of new technologies, or to meet the **market pull** of new consumer needs. In industry, this process of change is known as product development.

By adapting a product to meet a range of different needs, or in line with **technological advances**, a food manufacturer aims to make more profit.

A cottage pie is a simple product that contains a layer of minced beef in gravy and is topped with mashed potato. The case studies below show how this product can be adapted, using technological advances, or to meet the needs of different users.

Case study

Market push: New technologies

Cook-chill

Cook-chill cottage pies can be found on the refrigerated ready-meal shelves in most supermarkets.

Since the 1970s, food manufacturers have been developing food products that are made using the cook-chill process. This is when food is portioned into oven-ready containers and blast-chilled to preserve the goodness and flavour. Once chilled, the food can be stored for up to five days at a temperature below 5°C.

Using the cook-chill process means that food remains fresher for longer and looks more like it is homemade. The quality and appearance of cook-chill products is thought to be better than frozen products.

Textured vegetable protein (TVP)

TVP was actually invented in 1935, but was not commonly used in food products until much later. TVP is a meat substitute made from soya flour. TVP can be used in a cottage pie for the following reasons.

- To act as a substitute for minced beef, if you do not want the product to contain meat.

- To act as a **bulking agent**, so that less meat needs to be added. This would reduce the cost of ingredients.

Functional foods

As we become more health conscious, food manufacturers have begun to experiment with **functional food** ingredients. A functional food is a food that does more than simply provide the basic nutrients. It might contain extra nutrients, or claim to promote health or prevent disease.

One functional food that could be used in a cottage pie is an engineered minced beef. This is designed to be high in protein, with added omega-3 and vitamin B12. This would make the product more nutritious.

Case study

Market push: User needs

Vegetarians

A vegetarian cottage pie could be adapted by using TVP, as explained earlier. However, there are also other alternatives. For example, the beef could be replaced with a vegetable-based layer, or with pulses such as beans and lentils. The pulses would provide vegetarians with the protein that they might otherwise miss out on because they do not eat meat.

Low fat

To reduce the fat content in a cottage pie, a manufacturer could adapt it by using a leaner cut of meat, such as steak mince, rather than minced beef. Also, vegetables such as carrots and peas could be added to the meat layer to keep the expected texture but reduce the fat.

Luxury

Luxury ready-meals are relatively new to the market. They are normally sold at a higher price because of the ingredients they contain, and to make them stand out from cheaper alternative products.

A cottage pie in a luxury range would normally have extra ingredients such as wine, herbs and Worcester sauce added to the meat and gravy layer, to give it extra flavour.

It may also be sold in an ovenware dish to act as a **unique selling point** for its consumers.

Children

A cottage pie that is targeted at children could be adapted to contain more vegetables. These could even be pureed into the meat layer so they cannot be seen. It could also be served in a smaller sized portion, and even be presented in a novelty way, with a smiley face in the mashed potato for example.

Key terms

Market push: factors from within the industry that drive development, such as new technologies that manufacturers can take advantage of.

Market pull: demands from the market that drive change, such as the changing needs of the user.

Technological advances: newly discovered ways of doing things.

TVP: a meat substitute made from soya beans.

Bulking agent: a cheaper ingredient added to reduce the cost of making a product.

Functional food: food that has been designed to have extra health benefits.

Unique selling point: something that other products do not have.

Activities

1 Think about ways of developing another simple product to meet the four user needs: vegetarian, low fat, luxury and children.

2 What other users can you think of? How might you develop your product to meet their needs?

3 What technological developments do you think will affect food products in the future? Use your imagination to make some predictions.

Summary

- Products can develop over time with the introduction of new technologies, new materials and new manufacturing processes. This is called 'market push'.

- Products can also be developed in response to the needs of consumers. This is called 'market pull'.

Glossary

A

Additives: substances added to food products to preserve them or improve their colour, texture or taste.

Analyse: examine in detail and draw conclusions.

Anorexia: an illness where people do not eat enough.

Antibacterial solution: a liquid that can be sprayed on hands or surfaces to destroy bacteria.

Artificial additives: chemical substances added to food products to extend their shelf-life or improve their colour, texture or taste.

B

Bacteria: microscopic living things that live on everything around us.

Body Mass Index (BMI): a scale that tells you if you are a healthy weight for your height.

Bridge method: a method of cutting food safely, where your hand is held in a bridge shape.

Budget: a set amount of money you will allow yourself to spend on your shopping.

Bulking agent: a cheaper ingredient added to reduce the cost of making a product.

By-product: product created in the process of making something else.

C

Candied fruit: fruit soaked in sugar syrup to preserve it. For example, glace cherries.

Carbohydrates: foods that are based on starch, such as bread and potatoes.

Carotene: this is a yellow-orange pigment found in fruit and vegetables. It is converted in the body to vitamin A.

CHD: heart disease, usually caused by poor diet.

Claw method: a method of cutting food safely, where your hand is held in a claw shape.

Constraint: something that limits what you can design and make.

Consumer: the person who eats or purchases the food product.

Contaminated: when food contains something it should not contain: from bacteria to hair.

Criteria: properties that your product should have.

Cross-contamination: the transfer of food poisoning bacteria from one food to another.

Cultural diversity: celebrating different cultures and traditions.

D

Dairy foods: foods based on milk, usually from cows, which include butter, cheese and yoghurt.

Deficiency: when there is a shortage of a particular nutrient in the foods we eat.

Design brief: a short statement of what is required in a design.

Design process: a sequence of activities carried out to develop a product.

Diabetes: a condition where the body has difficulty converting blood sugar (glucose) to energy.

Dietary needs: the foods and nutrients that an individual needs to eat, or needs to avoid eating.

E

Empty calories: sugars that provide little or no nutrition, other than energy.

Energy expenditure: this is the amount of energy we use to make our muscles work.

Enrich: literally to make food richer. This can mean adding an ingredient, such as eggs, to add nutritional value to a food product.

Evaluate: compare something to a set of standards.

Evaluation: process of comparing something to a set of standards.

F

Factory farming: raising livestock in confined spaces, because it is cheaper and easier to control them.

Fairtrade: an organisation that makes sure food has been produced in a way that is sustainable and provides a future for the producers.

Flow chart: a sequence of events presented as a diagram.

Food miles: the distance food travels from the farm to your plate.

Freezer burn: grey patches on the outside of food caused by the evaporation of surface moisture. This happens if food is not packaged correctly in the freezer.

FSA: the Food Standards Agency: a government body set up to guide the public on food safety issues.

Fully automated: all of the process is done by machine.

Function: what the product is designed to do.

Functional food: food that has been designed to have extra health benefits.

Functional testing: testing by trying the product out, by tasting it, for example.

G

Gelatine: a glue-like substance that comes from animal bones and other animal tissues.

Genetically modified: food in which some genes have been altered in order to improve its properties.

H

Halal: meat eaten by Muslims. The animal is dedicated to Allah and the blood is drained away as part of the slaughtering process.

Hygienic: preparing and cooking food safely so it does not make anyone ill.

I

Imported: products brought from another country.

Impulse buys: unplanned, spur-of-the-moment purchases.

Inedible: cannot be eaten.

Inorganic: foods that have not been farmed according to the criteria for organic foods.

K

Kilocalories: the units used to measure the energy value of food.

Kosher: foods that have been approved for consumption by Jewish law.

L

Legal requirement: information that must be included by law.

Lifestyle: the kinds of activities done on a daily basis.

M

Manufactured: making a product to be sold.

Market: the group of potential customers who might buy a product.

Market pull: demands from the market that drive change, such as the changing needs of the user.

Market push: factors from within the industry that drive development, such as new technologies that manufacturers can take advantage of.

Modelling: making samples of a product for tasting and testing.

Monitor: watch constantly.

Multicultural society: a society where people from many faiths and countries of origin live together and share values and food choices.

N

Need: what the product you are designing must do.

Non-renewable resources: natural products that will eventually run out and cannot be replaced.

Novel foods: foods developed by humans.

Nutritional content: the amount of protein, fat, carbohydrate, vitamins and minerals that the product supplies.

O

Obesity: a medical condition where the body has too much fat, and health may suffer as a result.

Objective: based on facts rather than opinions.

Organic: foods that have been farmed in a sustainable and natural way, without the use of chemicals or artificial methods.

Organic farming: growing food and raising animals in a sustainable and natural way, without the use of chemicals or artificial methods.

P

Pasteurisation: heat treatment of milk to increase its shelf-life and make it safe to drink, without affecting its flavour.

Pathogenic bacteria: harmful bacteria that can cause food poisoning.

Perishable: fresh food that will only keep for a short time – fruit and vegetables, for example.

PIN: a method used to evaluate design ideas by considering: Positives, Improvements and Negatives.

Pollution: contamination of the environment.

Practical skills: the skills needed in order to cook a recipe.

Pre-manufactured: ready-made or processed, for example a ready-made pizza base.

Primary research: finding out the information you need by yourself.

Processed foods: bought products where raw ingredients are prepared, cooked and packaged ready to be eaten.

Processing: taking basic ingredients and changing them in some way to make them more useful, make them safer to eat, help them keep longer, or turn them into complete food products.

Production plan: the instructions for how to manufacture a product.

Product analysis: an existing product is evaluated as a form of research.

Product profile: a chart that displays the criteria of a product on a scale of 0–5. The aim is to get 5 out of 5.

Pulses: beans, peas and lentils. Foods that use pulses include chickpeas in houmous and kidney beans in chilli con carne.

Q

Questionnaire: a list of questions used to find out what lots of users want from the product.

R

Recycle: when a product is broken down to make a new product.

Reduce: use fewer resources to make the product, and produce less waste.

Refuse: do not accept things that are not the best choice for the environment.

Renewable resources: natural products that are replaced naturally and will not run out.

Repair: mending a product so that it lasts longer, or fixing an item when broken rather than throwing it away.

Research: gathering the information you need to be able to design the product.

Rethink: reconsider the design of the product and the way you use it.

S

Saturated fats: fats, usually from animal sources, that raise the cholesterol levels in the blood. This can lead to heart disease and other diseases.

Seasonal: food that has the best flavour and is most plentiful at a particular time of year.

Secondary research: finding out the information you need by using material that someone else has put together.

Semi-automated: some of the process is done by machine, but not all of it.

Sensory analysis: using the five senses to judge the appeal of a food product.

Sensory descriptors: words that describe the way foods affect our senses.

Shelf-life: the length of time stored food will keep its quality and be safe to eat.

Simmering: just below the boiling point of a liquid, when bubbles gently break the surface.

Specification: a list of needs that the product must meet.

Stabiliser: a substance added to foods that contain oil and water, to make sure that they stay mixed together properly.

Staple foods: these are the carbohydrate-based food products that are the main source of starch in a country's diet.

Starch: a type of carbohydrate that gives a slow release of energy.

Structure: the physical shape of a product.

Sustainable: having less impact on the environment.

Sustainable farming methods: those that have less impact on the environment.

Sustainable materials: materials that are easily available and can be harvested, manufactured and replaced using very little energy.

Sustainably: having less impact on the environment.

T

Tamper-proof packaging: designed so that you can see if someone has tried to open the product.

Technological advances: newly discovered ways of doing things.

Tender: easy to chew, not tough.

Tolerance: the amount of difference in size and thickness that is allowed when manufacturing a lot of the same product.

Tools: in Food Technology the pieces of equipment you use are sometimes called tools.

TVP: a meat substitute made from soya beans.

Unique selling point: something that other products do not have.

User: who the product is made for.

Vegan: someone who does not eat any animal products.

Want: features that you would like the product to have.

Y

Yield: the amount of food we can get from each plant.

Index